10-8

The Stories of Veteran Officer
W. Eli Lashe

Compiled and Expanded by
Ronald Gaines

ISBN: 978-0578177342

Papaw Publications USA
www.papawpublications.com

PP

INTRODUCTION

I first met Eli in February of 2003 on a deer hunting trip in the South Carolina low country.

I've always enjoyed telling and listening to a good story. But like most folks, mine are more embellished tales than anything else. Not so with Eli Lashe. His are the real deal.

Before an off-duty car accident in January of 1987 cost him most of his right leg and forced early retirement, his eight years with the Tuhont County Sheriff's Department (1963-1970); and fifteen with the Georgia State Patrol (1971-1986) proved a rich resource for stories about the best and worst in people.

But it wasn't just the stories, it's was how Eli told them – softly, incredibly detailed to be so many years removed – and void of pretentiousness. There's a simple candidness about them, especially those from his earliest years with Tuhont County – the ones I asked he include here.

Back in the 1960's, small-town, southern life was simpler in many ways. But be assured, those who sought to protect and serve on the local level encountered their share of the unexpected and out-of-the-ordinary.

I've attempted to recreate Eli's materials just as he prepared them, double-spacing, ragged alignment and all. He always used a typewriter (not much of a computer guy), saying he thinks best when sitting at his old Royal – the one he used to prepare countless reports. The comments for the back cover made it to me in long hand. As you've seen, that's how they were reproduced.

I wouldn't take anything for getting him to sit down and prepare them when he did. Shortly after he finished the project a sudden, severe illness took him from us.

As Eli requested, I pitched in and help write some of the more 'involved' sequences.

I've also taken the liberty of inserting a boxed-off comment here and there.

I hope you'll agree, having never done anything like this before, Eli did a good job writing stories from those early days he was 10-8.

Ron Gaines

Tuhont County Courthouse
1960

Spring 2014

Dear Reader:

As you might expect, this is new for me, and thinking about it brought several questions to mind.

The first is obvious: should I even undertake such a thing, having never written much more than incident reports? Given the support of Ron, my family, and several other good friends, I decided to give it a try.

There were other questions as well. Which would be most interesting? How much detail, and how graphic should they be? What I decided to do was tell it like it happened, with the help of my diary of course.

An interest in law enforcement started in my early years with the local newspaper. Covering the police docket put me in a position to meet officers around my hometown.

From time to time, invitations came to ride with members of the Asheford City Police Department, Tuhont County deputies, and once in a while, state troopers. Seeing their commitment to serve the public began to grow into an interest in law enforcement as a career.

It all came together in 1963. That was a big year in my life. On May 11th Millie and I got married. On July 26th I finished at the Georgia State Law Enforcement Academy, and in August I joined Tuhont County.

I did indeed type out (on my trusty old typewriter) the large majority of these stories. But I confess to asking Ron for help with some wording, titles, and general editing to get rid of my worst grammatical errors. Millie was a real help too.

Also, on things like radio traffic and fast-paced dialogue, I asked Ron to listen again to selected details and then write some sequences for me. I thought shifting gears from my basic, hunt-and-peck story-telling to a smoother presentation would help make a story easier to follow. You'll also see that I included a Disposition after each story, in which I briefly tell you what I remember happening with most of the people mentioned.

Many thanks to my family and friends for their encouragement, and to Millie, for her patience during all those re-writes. And thanks to each of you for your interest in my experiences during the years in which I tried to protect and serve.

Eli

CONTENTS

FRIDAY NIGHT FLIGHT
August 30, 1963

After visiting with folks standing near
the south end zone during the Tuhont-Lincoln
County High football game, Chief Deputy Dan
Simpson and I drove up SR 112 to the Tee Pee
Drive-In for a burger.

That Friday night was my first with the
department. Dan and I were in the county's new
Plymouth cruiser. We'd talked about the new-
car smell and watching as the first 100 miles
went on the speedometer. It was our newest and
nicest patrol unit.

As he always did, Dan turned around and
backed to the top of the sloped parking lot by
the building with the pointed roof - thus the
name, "Tee Pee". From there it was easier and
quicker to watch the road and get back on the
highway should we need to head out in a
hurry.

Dan insisted on buying my sandwich as he reached over and pinched the top of my shoulder. I told him he didn't need to do that but he insisted. He said something about the added expense of married life, before pulling four $3.00 dollar bills out of his pocket. Can you believe that; two hamburgers, two fries and two soft drinks for less than $3.00 dollars?

I've often thought Dan must have been thinking back on his first few days on the job - how he felt when everything was so new. Like me, he'd just turned 21 before starting with the Berryville, SC PD.

The couple of times I glanced over at Dan he was looking at me with that sort of crooked grin he had. He'd gone out of his way to make me feel welcome.

I knew he sincerely wished me well and was willing to help any way he could as I learned the ropes. It was a good few moments, but the mood was about to change.

Several folks told us later that the Galaxie was broadside when it came out of The Ranch House Restaurant. The way it sounded, I wouldn't doubt it.

One guy said tire smoke swung to the left and then to the right, back to the left and to the right again, chasing the rear bumper of Curly Epps' '63 Ford 500xl.

Thinking back on it, the cooler weather, the beginning of football season and a first-game win must have had all the high school kids feeling frisky. Curly Epps had every reason to be pumped up that night. He'd finally gotten Sheila Lattimore to take a ride. That was something the lanky redhead had worked on for quite a while.

The next few minutes proved tough for Dan. He and his wife, Trixie, had lived across the street from Sheila's parents, Parker and Pam Lattimore, for several. I really didn't know the Lattimores, but Dan knew Sheila to be a popular, attractive senior at Tuhont High.

Wiley Bunn was along for the ride - where he often was when a recent grad or upperclassman with a sexy ride made the rounds at the Ranch. Wiley didn't have a flashy car so he tried to hang around those who did. That night his tagalong ways would pay off in the worst sort of way.

I've always believed what we got into was something Curly had managed to avoid many times before - something he certainly didn't foresee, but many could have predicted.

That August had been a relatively quiet month on the county roads. But, my God, did we make up for lost time that Friday night.

It took only seconds for the roar of Epps' glasspacks, the squall of the oversized

[4]

rear tires and the salute of honking horns in the Ranch House parking lot to cover the 700-yards down State Highway 112 to our open windows.

Dan sprung into action. I confess that in those first few moments, I just tried to keep up with things. Whether you're in a patrol car, at a machine, or at a desk, I think most will agree there's nothing quite like a first day on the job.

Dan shouted "Here, hold this!", and tossed what remained of his hamburger in my direction. This is off the subject a bit, but I want to point out that the Tee Pee burgers had two patties - the first double-decker I can remember seeing, much less eating. There was something of a community-wide squabble as to which was better - the burgers or the barbeque. It was a dispute that continued until the Tee Pee burned down in the late '70's.

We both were looking up State Route 112 as Dan rolled the key to engage the Plymouth's classic starter. Another sidebar here: I always loved the sound of a Chrysler product cranking up. Others seemed to think they would have sold more cars if the starter didn't sound like a spinning top, but me, I sort of liked how they sounded.

The whirling whine was immediate and crisp on the new Fury Pursuit. Of course the starter was quickly drowned out by the growl of the throaty 383 Power Pack.

As I shuffled in the seat getting ready for what was likely to come, the remaining half of Dan's hamburger finished tumbling across my lap and over into the space between the door and my seat. That's also where I found the rest of mine later that night.

Dan left the lights off, including the red bubblegum machine up top and the alternating red and blue winkers, as he hustled the Fury down to the edge of the highway. I followed his lead in emptying what was left of my drink out the window and tossing the paper cup into the back seat.

Curly Epps was probably distracted by the striking blonde to his right; maybe he was again mesmerized by the power and harmonics when he really unleashed the 390; or it may simply have been his unfamiliarity with the county's new, black Plymouth that kept one of the county's top hot-rodders from checking out the Tee Pee parking lot coming up quickly on his left. More than likely it was a mix of the three. But I don't think Epps saw us until Dan hit the rack of lights.

At that point, Curly was still in 2nd gear. I'm sure he was flat-out. I had heard the several stories about Epps and his high-speed history, but I wasn't nearly as familiar as Dan with his past driving escapades.

Later our Chief Deputy told me Curly's response was what he knew it would be - knee-jerk and foolish.

In that flash of a moment, that instant, Curly chose to do what he'd done twice before. It was easy to visualize - him bouncing off the accelerator, popping the clutch, jerking the floor shift into third, burying the gas pedal a second time, and heading for the nearest turnoff from Highway 112.

Once before, he'd eluded Sheriff Earl Simpson, and he apparently thought he could do the same with the Sheriff's son. But Dan wasn't his father when it came to high speed pursuit, and the new, black Fury wasn't one of the county's three, chalky-white, under-powered, Belvederes.

The shock value really jumped when our headlights lit up the convertible.

Predictably, the top was down, and Sheila Lattimore's long, blonde, ponytail was blowing straight back.

When Curly came by, Wiley Bunn must have already dropped into the back floorboard. Neither one of us saw him.

———··———

"My God, I think that was Sheila Lattimore in there with him! Curly, you crazy fool!" exclaimed Simpson, a vision of his seven-year-old, twin girls flashing through his mind.

Other thoughts were also in the deputy's head as he re-pressed the transmission button to confirm it was fully seated in drive mode.

…just before 11:00 o'clock on a Friday night, and he's pullin' a stunt like that between the Ranch House and the Tee Pee…that boy's learned nothin' from his court appearances.

"Make sure your seatbelt's good and tight, Eli! Don't know if this guy's got enough sense to stop before it's too late."

[9]

"I've already tightened her down, Dan!" replied the new deputy as he instinctively pulled a third time on the nylon belt.

———···———

As we both watched the headlights bounce on the accelerating Ford, my feelings were doing some bouncing of their own, between anger and fear. I felt anger over Curly's thoughtless actions and fear of what may lie ahead for many people.

The Ford was over the hill and a half mile in front of us before we were confident that a pickup heading south on 112 was going to slow down.

I remember shouting, "He's stoppin'! He's stoppin'! Let's go, Dan!"

Dan pulled out into the highway and opened the Fury's 4-barrel. Man, did it jump. I don't remember for sure, but I believe it had well over 300 horsepower. It was a beast and likely a real match for the Galaxie with its similar engine. I don't remember anything about gearing and such, but the Plymouth was strong on the top end.

As the new, black Pursuit wound out, we both rolled up the front windows and slid back on the bench seat. I'm not sure whether my legs or the Plymouth did more to drive me into the seatback. I remember looking for the just-right-distance to set my legs and feel braced.

Dan pitched his hat into the back seat. I didn't know why that night, but I did the same. Several days later I asked why he'd tossed his hat in the back. Since it had fallen down on the bridge of his nose in a chase two years earlier, Dan said he'd made it a practice to put several feet between his eyes and the campaign hat. For the rest of my county and highway patrol days, I followed the practice.

———...———

"Call it in, Eli!"

The new deputy reached for the dash and the heavy, metal mic on the two-way.

"1662 to Asheford," said Lashe with a bounce in his voice as the Plymouth left the sharp rise in SR 112 a full 6-inches off the ground.

The Tuhont County deputy had driven in many pursuits, and his reputation for success was widely known. He was good, but he would have been the first to say running down the powerful, fleeing Ford and its panicked driver would be both dicey and dangerous.

"Go ahead, '62", replied radio operator Glen Evans from the Georgia State Patrol radio room in Asheford. Sharing the same frequency on what was called the "low band"; area counties routed much of their radio traffic through the twenty-four-hour patrol barracks.

"Asheford, we're in pursuit of a red Ford Galaxie convertible heading south on State Route 112, about two miles below the Tee Pee Drive-In," said Lashe, holding the Motorola's mic close to his mouth in an attempt to overcome wind and engine noise swirling in the cruiser.

"10-4, '62......we have a unit in the south end of the county. Stand by one." The long-time operator moved to the state band radio and called Corporal William Moon.

"Asheford to 7-12."

As usual, when Billy Moon was at the wheel, the reply came quickly.

[12]

"Go ahead, Asheford," answered the Corporal, who was headed north on County Road 2234, approximately ten-miles south of 1662's location.

"7-12, the county is in pursuit of a red Ford convertible heading south on 112. Be advised that the pursuit is coming toward you at a very high rate of speed. Are you able to assist?"

There was little hesitation.

"10-4....I'll get over on 112 and contact the county unit directly. Who is it, Asheford?"

"It's 1662."

"10-4," replied Moon as he turned left onto Carroll Lane, a dirt road connecting CR 2234 and SR 112. In a matter of moments, Moon reached the state highway, spraying gravel as he turned right and headed north toward the unfolding pursuit.

———···———

As the state unit was heading toward us we reached the Cannon Creek Bridge. Looking down the long straight stretch, Dan and I could tell we had closed on the Ford when the large, round, tail lights lit-up under hard breaking. We could see he was slowing to make a right turn on Chapman Road.

By then we knew Epps had no intention of stopping.

I was thinking just how frightened Sheila Lattimore must be. From what Dan Simpson knew and later told me about Sheila, the terrifying ride would have been something she'd never have agreed to. Neither one of us knew much about Wiley Bunn. But he must have been beyond scared as well.

Things were happening and decisions were being made at break-neck speed.

————···————

Lashe raised the mic to his lips with an update. "Okay, Asheford, he's turning right on Chapman, heading toward Cedar Row."

"10-4, '62. You get that 7-12?"

Corporal Moon didn't reply directly to Evans' question. His next transmission provided the answer. "1662, this is 7-12. I'm taking a left onto CR 2420, headed to Cedar Row…should be there in five or six minutes."

"10-4, 7-12….Asheford we might oughta advise Cedar Row PD what's headed their way…you been able to do so?"

"62 I've tried twice…no response…might be a little late for those boys to be out and about."

Dan Simpson shook his head, while Lashe replied simply, "10-4 on that."

———…———

I remember Chapman Road had been recently paved by the county. It was straight and pretty smooth, only a little less conducive to high speed than 112 had been.

I can surely tell you this; we were haulin' it. The new Pursuit was clearing most of the bumps. But the few we felt made the Fury's stiffened suspension shutter, us too. It seems to me now that we must have been floating about as much as we were rolling.

I know each time the cruiser wiggled over the highest ripples in Chapman, the tension rose for me. Dan didn't say it or show it, but I'll bet the same was true for him.

[15]

That's about the time I can remember thinking — Oh, come on Epps! Slow down, before somebody gets hurt, you crazy punk! Believe I was more angry than frightened at that point.

———··———

"Okay, 7-12.....it looks like this subject has no intention of slowing down...what's ya 20?

Moon was in his fourth year at the Asheford Georgia State Patrol post and very familiar with Curly Epps and his fire-engine-red convertible. He'd ticketed him once in the souped-up Chevy Biscayne his father traded in on the Galaxie several months earlier.

"'62, I'm about two miles southeast of Cedar Row." There was a brief pause before Moon keyed the mic again. He already knew the answer but thought he might ask anyway.

"We chasing Curly Epps, I guess?"

As all three cars rocketed toward the Cedar Row Community, Eli replied; "10-4! It's him again!"

Comment: On several occasions I've heard Eli talk about what he called the classic, muscle-car protocol playing out that Friday night in the southern end of Tuhont County — powerhouse cars, youthful, often immature drivers ready to take on the law, and officers dealing with the unnerving reality that enforcing it often took place at death-defying speeds.

———··———

[16]

We found out later Sheila had been crying and begging Epps to stop since the Ford passed the Tee Pee. Maybe it was the warning Epps had been given the last time he went before Judge Albert Wells that out-weighed Sheila's pleas.

Immature and short on judgment, at least at that moment, I guess Epps must have been savvy enough to know the difference between traffic violations and full-blown felonies. I'm sure of one thing; his thoughts that night were more about himself than anyone else.

What's often crossed my mind when thinking about that Friday night are the bad consequences which can follow even the shortest flash of immaturity or lack of judgment behind the wheel.

Even at 21-years-old, Epps was too immature to consider the greater likelihood of a manageable outcome, had he simply gotten on the brakes, pulled in at the Tee Pee and offered an apology for the showy exit from the Ranch House. Rather his actions left him facing the challenge of apologizing to two nervous, angry officers following miles of nerve-racking pursuit.

What is it that's said today? The cover-up is always worse than the crime? I suppose that's equally true when even a brief hot-rodding infraction is judged against the dangers of an extended, violation-filled attempt to run.

———···———

"Curly, come on man, you've gotta stop. You're gonna kill us!" screamed Wiley Bunn from the back seat.

"One more time, you guys, shut up! I can't afford to get caught again! I know what I'm doin'! I can get away from these guys! One more turn, and we've got it made."

———···———

Dan and I didn't know it as we neared Cedar Row, but Epps had a plan. He was thinking about the partially-completed extension of the Asheford bypass.

Paving had gotten to the new Chapman Road Bridge. But beyond the bridge, heading on down to where the bypass was going to merge back into 112, only clearing and rough grading had been done. And that's where Curly was headed.

He later told the court his intention was to kill his lights, take the exit up to the bridge, turn left, and head down the unpaved roadbed. Had his lead, the curves and resulting lines-of-sight on Chapman worked out, he might have pulled it off.

——— ··· ———

"1662, I just turned right at the red light in Cedar Row and am headed east back toward you on Chapman."

"10-4, 7-12, we're a mile from the bypass construction. That puts us about four miles apart," responded Lashe.

"Here, let me speak to him, Eli," said Dan Simpson, reaching for the mic.

"7-12, if you're not there yet, how 'bout pullin' in on your right at Dooley's Store. Maybe all your lights and seeing a second vehicle involved, Epps will think better of continuing with this! If he doesn't stop, we might oughta break it off before something bad happens," radioed Simpson, growing increasingly-flustered with the situation.

Corporal Billy Moon saw the headlights dancing as the car rounded the curve two-hundred yards west. Every red light he had was winking when he pulled forward slightly, only to see the county's Plymouth flash by.

[19]

"7-12, he come by you?" asked the Chief Deputy.

"No '62 you're the only thing to come by me."

"Eli, you see anything I missed?"

"No, Dan, he went into that curve when you were talking to Moon and I didn't see him after that."

———··———

I remember with all that power and the new rubber we almost went over when Dan spun the Fury in the road. Believe that was when the rest of the double-decker hamburger left my lap and joined up with Dan's down between my seat and door.

When we got back to Dooley's Store, Billy Moon was already well ahead of us heading west on Chapman. He was probably as keyed up as we were.

I think it was Moon that first suggested Curly must've gotten off at the bypass. I wasn't sure about that; the whole area was pretty heavily under construction and it figured to be particularly dangerous at night. But with Curly Epps, who knew what to expect.

While Billy checked the roadsides for skid marks a half-mile back from the bypass, Dan and I went up the partially-paved exit ramp and stopped.

The pavement butted up against the bridge in front of us, and Dan used his A-post spotlight to confirm it hadn't gone beyond the bridge. At first, I don't think we said a word as Dan twisted his spot to the south and I wrenched mine up the pavement to my right.

I remember Dan's question. It was simple and to the point: "Where the hell did that peckerwood go?"

It was the first time I'd heard the word, "peckerwood". Don't remember hearing or saying it before that night, but I've sure added it to my lexicon since.

Just after Dan posed the question, my spotlight hit the eyes of a deer running across the pavement about 50 to 60 yards up the bypass. I'm sure enough glad I didn't shout out something that would've sent us chasing after that animal.

It's a wonder I didn't, as wired and drenched in adrenalin as I was. And, you know what? I'll bet even a veteran like Dan Simpson would've swung that Plymouth to the right before I finished getting the words out of my mouth.

We both wanted to get our hands on Curly Epps in the worst sort of way.

About that time Corporal Moon's headlights hit our rearview mirrors.

I recall 7-12 was light blue. I don't know where that came from, but the long, 4-door Bonneville was baby blue. Don't recall ever seeing another GSP car that color, before or since.

Dan and I watched in our respective rearviews as Billy got out and walked up on the driver's side of the Fury. Dan's window was already down.

And, you know why?

He'd rolled it down to spit, just before Moon walked up.

I've always wondered how Dan Simpson was able to do that. There wasn't enough moisture left in my entire body to muster up a good spit, much less in my mouth.

———···———

"Dan, you guys see anything?"

"No. But he had to come up here and go one way or the other. We backed down a minute ago and eased back up the ramp, looking for tire or skid marks. We didn't see anything."

Just as Simpson finished speaking, Moon put his hand on the chief deputy's shoulder and straightened up.

"Wait. You hear that?"

Simpson got out of the car. Lashe was already standing in the open door on the opposite side. Again, the three drew still and listened, with only Moon having some sense of the direction from which the sound had come.

The next time all three heard the shouts and crying.

"It's in front of us, Dan! It's in front of us!" shouted Billy Moon before he and Simpson broke into a run in the headlights stretching across the fresh concrete. They were headed toward the opposite exit ramp. Eli Lashe was close behind.

———··———

The first thing we saw, about two-thirds of the way down the other ramp grading was the rear end of the Ford raised up about two feet off the ground. The lights were on; the radio was blaring; the engine was still running; and the driver's door was open. As we slowed, we heard what sounded like a male yelling and a female's cries for help.

Epps was leaning to the left of the steering wheel with a lot of blood around his shoulders and down the back of the

[24]

sweatshirt he was wearing. For a moment we couldn't tell if he was dead or alive. Billy Moon went to him first. I stepped behind Moon and leaned over his left shoulder.

Dan went around to Sheila, who was definitely alive. She was over against the passenger door sobbing and begging for help with her lower back.

The second time Moon spoke to Epps, Curly sat up and threw his head back. We could see he was busted up and hear him raising hell with every breath. But he was alive. Both Moon and Dan grabbed their two-way radios to call for help. Corporal Moon beat Dan to the button.

I suppose the first real mistake I made working for the Tuhont County Sheriff's Department was leaving my two-way in the front seat of that Plymouth.

I'd been around many auto accidents before that night, but I hadn't even begun to hone the automatic responses of a good patrol officer - those instinctual moves like grabbing your two-way when you leave the patrol car at an active scene. I was probably fortunate to have remembered my flashlight, even in the dark.

———— ··· ————

"7-12 to Asheford...!"

"Go ahead 12," came Glen Evans' quick reply.

"Asheford, subject has wrecked at the intersection of Chapman Road and the bypass just east of Cedar Row. 10-52 as quickly as possible."

"10-4, I'll advise when emergency services are on the way. You gonna need one or more med vehicles?"

"We'll need two, Asheford. Send us two!"

Curly Epps was pushing Lashe and Moon away from the driver's door, insisting that he be permitted to get out of the car.

"Get out of my way! I smell gas man! This thing might blow up," shouted Epps as he snatched at the single-strap seatbelt with his right hand and pressed against his nose and mouth with his left.

About that time both Lashe and Moon whiffed the gas — faint but definitely in the air. Both moved from urging Epps to remain still to assisting him out of the front seat. The scent of hot metal mixed with that of dripping coolant and gasoline to create the smell so familiar to early responders on the scene of an automobile accident. Before Lashe reached in and switched off the engine, the chance of a fire was a legitimate concern.

In short order, Curly Epps was out of the car and sitting on the ground well back up the exit ramp grade. He continued to rock back and forth, using his hands and shirttail in an attempt to slow the blood pouring from his face.

Eli joined Simpson in trying to care for Sheila Lattimore, who'd gone from screaming and crying to a constant moan punctuated by whimpers and soft calls for her mother and father.

Curly's broken nose, busted lips and several broken teeth was one thing, but Lattimore's persistent agony from what looked to be a lower spinal issue was something else entirely.

The officers didn't dare try to move her.

"Sheila, can you hear me, honey? This is Dan Simpson, your neighbor, can you hear me?" asked the veteran deputy as he tried gently to stabilize the girl and keep her from leaning further to the right out the passenger door he'd just eased open.

"Dan, you think we should loosen her seatbelt?"

[27]

"Don't think so, Eli. I watched her try and move her legs to adjust her position and that didn't look good. I'm just afraid to do much until the meds get here."

There was little more the officers could do but wait for the ambulances. That made the next call from Glen Evans particularly welcome.

"Asheford to 7-12."

"Go ahead Asheford," replied Moon who was standing just behind Curly Epps, twenty yards up the incline.

"Two ambulances are on the way. Their ETA is eight to ten minutes."

"10-4 Asheford, we need them as soon as possible."

"They've been advised the situation is urgent."

———··———

I don't really remember what I did until the meds arrived. I do remember the two ambulances got there within seconds of one another, both coming west on Chapman, driving up the exit ramp and across the pavement to within feet of the convertible.

All four attendants helped get Sheila out of the Ford, onto a wheeled stretcher and into one of the Knolton Funeral Home medical

[28]

conversions. Following crying and tears when she was removed from the seat, she'd grown quiet, almost unresponsive. I remember looking at her right eye. It was grotesquely swollen and the strange angle of her left hand looked as though her wrist was broken.

That night Epps was belligerent with everyone that represented any form of authority. Even bloody and perhaps deserving of some sympathy, he was tough to take, cursing and promising bad things for everyone when his father found out how long it had taken for the ambulances to arrive.

Locally, Asa Epps, Sr. was a well-connected and powerful man, whose potential for political retaliation was something Curly often mentioned when wanting his words to have added impact. It's one of the things that added to his bigshot reputation.

While we were waiting on the wrecker, Moon, Dan and I looked over the scene in hopes of figuring out what had happened. There was no mystery.

Epps had badly misjudged his speed before reaching the top of the exit ramp. A turn wasn't an option. So, he simply continued straight across and down the opposite exit ramp. That was likely the best of his options. But, there was a surprise waiting. The far ramp hadn't been paved.

And far worse than that, there was a 2-foot wide, 3-foot deep trench across the dirt incline where a pipe for the drainage system was to be buried. The short skid marks indicated he hadn't done much in the way of stopping before the nose and front wheels went into the culvert.

His speed was estimated at 40 to 50 miles per hour. He'd probably wanted to stay off the brakes so we wouldn't see the taillights.

It must have been quite a jolt.

But, mentally at least, there was another jolt in store for two unsuspecting Tuhont County deputies and one GSP corporal.

———··———

Things had calmed down as the wrecker was finally hooked up to the Galaxie's rear axle and the Ford pulled back out of the ditch. When the four flood lights on top of the tow vehicle lit up the dash and inside of the windshield, Simpson and Lashe saw the same thing at the same time.

"Wait! Hold it a minute!" shouted Eli, throwing his left arm and hand into the air toward the wrecker. He stepped to the passenger's side of the car and leaned over the passenger door.

"What the hell's that?" asked Eli, putting his flashlight beam directly onto the material at the right lockdown latch for the canvas roof. Lashe's eyes offered a partial answer – an answer that was chilling.

The hair was easily recognized, but a closer look was needed to confirm the scalp and other matter

wedged into the canvas roof's chrome locking
mechanism.

————— ··· —————

I moved my flashlight and saw the shoe.
The black floor mat had swallowed up the
black loafer. In all sincerity, the shock was
overwhelming. It was the first time any of us
had thought about the possibility of someone
being in the back seat.

As I recall, the '63 Galaxie 500's came
with seatbelt attachment hardware already
installed, both front and back. However, it was
up to the owner to decide whether they would
install the belts themselves. Most owners
choose to install lap restraints, but in the
front only. Curly's father had chosen that
half-way option.

The front belts clearly played a
helpful role, but, that night, anyone in the
back was looking at something terrible. When
the Ford dove into the open trench, the small-

framed high school junior, Wiley Bunn, was catapulted into and over the front windshield, across the hood and head-first into a pile of cement pipe stacked on the right of the exit way, some 30-feet below the ditch.

First the windshield and then the beveled edges at the end of the pipes inflicted terrible damage. His body had come to rest between the triangular stack of pipe and the excavated bank to the right.

Dan and I rolled several of the pipe sections away, and stood looking at the wreck's third victim.

Billy Moon was already on the way to answer another call. Both ambulances were gone, and the on-lookers had dwindled down to nearly nothing. There was only me, Dan, the wrecker driver still in the truck up the hill, and Wiley Bunn's body covered from the waist up by Dan's dark blue, London Fog jacket.

I remember feeling like I'd been gut-punched.

With only two $1.00 dollar bills in his pocket and no identification of any kind, Dan and I knew only one thing for sure about 1:00 AM on August 31, 1963 - things had gotten much worse for Asa Epps, Jr.

DISPOSITION

Wiley Bunn's father was killed in World War II and his mother pasted away shortly thereafter. There was only his grandmother, with whom Wiley lived, to deeply grieve his death. That she did. I really don't remember how it came together, but Billy Moon, Dan Simpson and I attended his funeral. It just seemed like something we should do.

I can't tell you the specifics of <u>Sheila</u> <u>Lattimore's</u> injuries, but I do remember the doctors were very concerned with some things in her lower back. There were two surgeries - one on an eye socket and the other on her spine. The last I knew she'd recovered and married Wade Smart's pharmacist-son. They moved somewhere in Tennessee.

<u>Corporal Billy Moon</u> received a promotion shortly after the first of the year (1964) and transferred to one of the Atlanta-area posts as Sergeant William Moon.

And, of course there's <u>Curly Epps</u> - more on him in the next story.

NEW DUDS AND DUE DELIBERATION
November - January 1963-64

There are two reasons I wanted to include this story: first, it's an obvious follow up to the one you just read; and second it's a clear example of how law enforcement frustrations go well beyond a nerve-racking moment on the road.

Curly Epps' trial was gaveled to order on Wednesday, November 27th - five days after the assassination of President Kennedy. The nation was deeply stunned and distraught. Most things were knocked off kilter a bit, including many local legal institutions. The trial had been scheduled to start on Monday, the 25th.

Following the wreck, Curly spent several weeks in the hospital, where repair work was done on his face. I remember someone saying he have had a brain transplant while he was in there.

Curly was looking at a string of charges - speeding, failure to stop for an officer, a list of traffic violations, etc. But the big one was vehicular manslaughter. In some states it's called vehicular homicide.

Depending on the circumstances, which ran from basic to gross negligence, on through a reckless disregard for others' safety, the penalty handed down in '63 could range from 1 to 20-years in prison.

With the possible exception of Curly himself, everyone knew it was serious business, none more than Curly's well-to-do father, Asa, Sr.

Mr. Epps had gotten his youngest son out of a variety of binds on a variety of occasions. As expected, he got the ball rolling to do it again well before Curly got out of the hospital.

In October he hired a high-powered
attorney from Atlanta - Darwin Corvello. I'd
never heard of him, but my superiors said he
had quite a reputation. For the Epps trial he
brought along only one associate, an
attractive younger-than-might-be-expected
blonde whose name I don't remember and didn't
have in my diary.

Corvello was a slick customer - the first
guy I ever saw that wore custom-made suits.
The fact was, in 1963, I'd never heard of a
custom-made suit, much less seen someone that
wore two or three in a single week.

Comment: Don't let Eli come across as too much of a bumpkin
here. He's a sharp dresser now, and I'll bet his uniforms and
leather were always kept in first-class condition at both the
county and state level.

Everyone wondered, often out loud, just
how much he was paid. Whatever it was, Asa
Epps got his money's worth and Curly got no
less than he'd come to expect - daddy to the
rescue.

[39]

Curly's father was a player in and
around Asheford. Of course I don't remember
the exact number, but he certainly employed
over 2,000 people in his Georgia and South
Carolina textile operations. Everyone knew he
would do all within his power to get Curly
out of the trouble he was in.

The prosecution was handled by Gus
Mena. He'd grown up in Tuhont County, run for
local office on two occasions and won both
times. Gus was well-thought-of, both
personally and professionally.

Of course nothing about his dress or
manner rivaled Corvello, but he was not to be
taken lightly. Over several years, I came to
know him as a generally soft-spoken man,
well-read and more than a cut above average
when it came to arguing the law. I would
describe him as what most folks might

envision when they talk about a true southern gentleman.

Whenever I think about Gus, I always think of his handsome handlebar mustache, and how well it matched his thick white hair. I don't think I ever saw him that I wasn't reminded of Mark Twain.

I never really knew Asa Epps, Sr. but on one occasion I heard a county official describe his involvement in local power politics as "mostly behind the scenes".

When you coupled those words with the shallow smile that followed, the clear implication was that Asa Epps, Sr. was a man who could make things happen one way or the other.

Of course I was called to testify on behalf of the prosecution, as was Dan Simpson and Bill Moon. Just about everyone in the county was deeply interested in the high-profile proceedings.

Simpson, Moon and I related the night's events as accurately as possible - how it started, what took place each moment at high speeds and how it ended.

I thought Dan's testimony was particularly good in describing the feeling of helplessness that must have terrorized Curly's passengers. On the stand, Sheila Lattimore had already provided a clear picture of the panicked begging Epps chose to ignore.

Dan painted a brief but moving picture of both the manner and moment of Wiley Bunn's death.

Gus Mena did a masterful job of asking questions that guided our testimony in hopes of bringing the jury along on that terrible ride. In addition, he emphasized Curly Epps' previous violations and the need to think of the ought-to-know-better 21-year-old as a recurrent offender.

To further outline Curly's past driving violations, Mena called Deputy Renea Raney from the records department to summarize the defendant's driving history. She presented information on behalf of Tuhont County, the city and the Georgia State Patrol.

Her responses to the prosecutor's questions made two things clear: Epps' violations were both numerous and serious. In addition, she sounded personally offended - both as an officer and as a citizen. As I remember, many of us thought at the time many of her responses to Mena's questions were overdone.

    a. 5 citations for speeding, one for 65 in a 20-mph school zone (3 by Tuhont

County and 1 each by the city and
state)

b. 3 for reckless driving (all by Tuhont
County)

c. 2 for drag racing on public roads (1
by Tuhont County and 1 by the
Georgia State Patrol)

d. 1 for failing to stop for an officer
involving high-speed pursuit (Tuhont
County after which his driving
license was suspended for 6 months)

e. And, 1 citation for driving without a
license (Georgia State Patrol)

On the morning Curly's attorney cross
examined Raney, I happened to be standing in
the back of the courtroom with Asheford PD
Sgt. Larry Perryman. Larry was a bright guy,
who had intensions of becoming an attorney.
He was taking night classes toward that end.

Just after Gus finished questioning Renea, Larry leaned over and whispered -- Mena didn't need Raney to show that bad attitude and tone toward Epps.

———..———

Corvello started in his usual, measured tone. He spoke and moved like a viper just before it strikes.

"Good morning, Officer Raney."

"Good morning," replied Renea, as she leaned back in her chair, seeming to want as much distance between herself and Darwin Corvello as possible.

The attractive, twenty-six-year-old was completing her first six months with the department. She'd never testified in court, and Corvello's demeanor clearly intimidated her.

"I think we all can see you're battling a terrible cold this morning. Let me join Mr. Mena in thanking you again for being here to help us delve into some things."

Raney offered a quick nod, before Corvello responded with a condescending smile, before slowly lowering his head and shuffling a single sheet of paper. While he looked at the notes in front of him, Corvello offered up several moments of silence. It was effective.

"Deputy Raney, how long have you worked in records for Tuhont County?"

"Six months," replied the county's only female deputy.

"And, the job in records is the only position with the department you've held, isn't that correct?"

Raney glanced quickly at Gus Mena before answering, "That's right."

"You've never been part of a pursuit; never dealt with the emotions that are part of such an experience; in fact, you've never even made an arrest, isn't that right, Deputy Raney?"

Gus Mena came to his feet, slowly shaking his head as so many had seen him do when he wished to appear confounded by the content of opposing counsel's question.

"Your honor, it was stipulated in the beginning that Deputy Raney worked in records and she's testified that her responsibilities have been confined to that important area of the department's operations. I'm wondering if there's a point at the end of Mr. Corvello's inquiry into the obvious."

Judge Theo Elston used the edge of the bench to pull himself forward in his black leather chair. He had a reputation for moving slowly, appearing detached, if not wearied, by much of what took place in his court.

His reply to Mena's objection was more a confession than a procedural correction: "Mr. Corvello, I was wondering the same thing."

"Certainly, Judge. I was just thinking about how incensed officer Raney seemed to be with Mr. Epps' driving record....calling it "egregious", without having the perspective of a single traffic stop, much less over-the-road experiences that might justify such scorn."

No one could say anything before Darwin Corvello hurried off to the next question.

"Deputy Raney, I believe you have Mr. Epps' folder there in front of you, right?"

"Yes, I do."

"Would you refer to the paperwork and tell the court Mr. Epps' age when each of the violations you've mentioned occurred."

Raney started to fumble through the file, looking more befuddled than she'd been since taking the stand. After several moments she looked up from her lap. "Sir, that may take a few minutes, since I will need to scan several folders. There's more than one form here and I'll have to find the age notation on each."

"Well, let me help you," responded Corvello, taking a note from his co-counsel. His age ranged from sixteen to eighteen, with the average being seventeen-point-three years when cited – not even the legal age of eighteen."

"Deputy, don't you think that should have been called to the court's attention by you or Mr. Mena when you were emphasizing his "egregious" driving? He was a teenager!"

Before Raney could fashion any sort of answer, Darwin Corvello ended the cross-examination; "No further questions."

Gus Mena was quickly to his feet for a second time; "Re-direct your honor."

"Go ahead, Mr. Mena," replied Judge Elston.

"Deputy Raney, what was Asa Epps' age the night Wiley Bunn was thrown from that speeding car and killed?"

"Mr. Mena, he was twenty-one-years-old."

"Twenty-one years old! Yes, he was indeed. Thank you, Deputy Raney."

———··———

During the lunch break, Larry Perryman and I ate a hotdog at the Dog House. We talked about a lot of things. But the one thing I remember for sure was Larry's comments about the driving record and how it appeared to him the defense wasn't taking it seriously enough.

It was his opinion that Corvello was going to defend the case in an unexpected way. He didn't think arguing against a questionable driving record would be the direction Corvello's team would take.

My goodness was Perryman right!

[48]

Corvello put one central question before the court: just how much responsibility do officers bear for engaging in and continuing with high-speed pursuits? He focused in on the proposition that a simple decision to break off the chase would have saved Wiley Bunn's life and avoided Sheila Lattimore's suffering.

The notion took Gus Mena by surprise. I know it was the first time most of us had ever really thought about such a thing. From the exchange of glances you could tell the jury was shocked, but taken by the idea.

Over the next few days Corvello called and Gus Mena cross-examined several witnesses as to the number and nature of traffic deaths associated with high-speed pursuit. Gus did a good job re-grouping and attempting to head-off the defense's unexpected direction. But it was obvious Corvello was well-prepared.

The jury was wrestling with the implications of the carefully-crafted question and its impact on the notion of ultimate responsibility. It was Corvello's final surprise witness that sealed the deal and proved devastating for the prosecution.

———— ⋯ ————

"Would you state your name for the court please?"

"Glen Evans."

"And, what type of work do you do, Mr. Evans?"

"I'm a radio operator with the state patrol."

"How long have you done that sort of work, sir?"

"Just under ten years."

"Operator Evans, you were working the post's low-band radio the night officers Simpson and Lashe were chasing my client, isn't that correct?"

"Yes, that's right."

"It's my understanding that you can monitor the conversation between cars on your radio system. Am I correct in that, sir?"

"Yes, we are able to hear transmissions car-to-car."

"At one point in the chase did Deputy Simpson speak with your state unit number 7-12, which had switched over to the low-band frequency while attempting to help the two deputies in the pursuit?"

"He did. Trooper Moon had moved to head off the car Dan Simpson was chasing."

"And, just outside of Cedar Row, did Deputy Simpson express concern that the pursuit may well end badly?"

Evans paused several seconds, before answering simply, "Yes,"

"As best you can, would you please tell the court what Deputy Simpson said to Corporal Moon that night?"

"I don't remember exactly, but he said something like, 'we might oughta break this off before something bad happens'."

"And, by the word 'this', you took him to mean the hot pursuit, is that correct?"

"Mr. Corvello, I don't know what else he could have meant," barked Evans – for the first and only time showing frustration with the awkward, strained situation.

———··———

Folks said Glen Evans never once looked at Dan Simpson, who was in the courtroom that day.

In that trial, there were two firsts for me: an introduction to custom-tailored suits and the far-more haunting notion that culpability could be directed toward officers involved in hot pursuit.

Today, you'd be hard-pressed to find a jurisdiction where hot pursuit isn't severely restricted by policy or forbade by law.

DISPOSITION

I only saw Asa Epps, Sr. three or four times after the trial. It's the first time I remember most. In the week after the trial Sheriff Simpson and I were standing in the courthouse parking lot when a black Chrysler Imperial pulled up and the rear window went down. Epps smirked (smirked, not smiled), tipped his hat, and powered the window back up. Sheriff Earl was a church-goin' man, but that day, mostly under his breath, he back-slid a bit.

Curly Epps was found guilty. He lost his license for two years and went on probation for the same period. He served no time for his lethal actions in late August of 1963. Of course, he did receive a real "talking too" from Judge Theo Elston. Curly finally got into a scrape his father couldn't get him out of. He was shot to death in a Nevada brothel in the late 1970's.

Judge Elston built quite a home somewhere in the mountains of Western North Carolina. He retired there two years after the trial. It would be safe to say his retirement seemed sudden, at least unexpected. He told folks it was for health reasons.

And here's the other interesting twist following that trial. Glen Evans resigned from the state patrol, effective immediately. A good friend said he bought a right nice boat and coastal home in the Naples, FL area. The same friend said he walked away from most of what he'd accrued with the state. Perhaps he no longer needed it. It's always made me wonder just what did go on - "mostly behind the scenes".

Darwin Corvello and his young, female associate walked out of the courtroom after the trial, and as far as I know, no one around Asheford had further dealings with the firm.

Gus Mena practiced law well into the 1980's, winning more trials than he lost. The last I heard he was ailing and living in his daughter's garage apartment somewhere in Alabama. His wife passed away shortly after the Epps trial.

I know Larry Perryman did manage to pass the bar exam. For several years he practiced law with the firm Gus Mena co-founded in Asheford back in the early '50's.

THE WILLET WARS
June, 1964

In early June, 1964, I'd been with Tuhont
County for about 10 months, and I was
beginning to get my feet on the ground. All my
colleagues were helpful in my efforts to do
so - all but one - Avery Cooley.

Avery was well over 6 feet tall, thick
and broad-shouldered. Even when he'd just
shaved it looked like he needed to try again.
His build, deep-set eyes, black hair and dark
coloration only added to his gruff look.

In the beginning, the rub with Avery
bothered me quite a bit. I'd quickly grown
comfortable with all my fellow officers and
the office staff, but not with Cooley. It wasn't
something that kept me up at night, but it did
strike a sour note every time he responded to
a "good morning" with little more than a
grunt.

[55]

Several others told me to just ignore it, saying Avery had always done his job well - working the front office and helping with various jailer duties - but when it came to one-on-one he wasn't going to win a personality contest.

I suppose it was his difficulty in getting along with others was what kept him off the road. After all, Sheriff Earl Simpson wasn't just in the business of law enforcement; he also had to remember the political side of things. Having a deputy that found it difficult to smile and shake a hand wasn't the best way to earn and keep votes.

I didn't know it in the beginning, but Avery and I were going to get on better terms, under the worst of circumstances. The improved relationship was to be a by-product of the "Willet Wars".

On June 12, 1964, Millie was spending the weekend with her mom and dad and I was scheduled to be off. After getting some dinner, I stopped by the office. I don't remember why, just didn't want to hurry back to that empty house I guess.

Next to Dan Simpson, Tate Taft had become my best friend on the job. He had an infectious laugh, and a confident approach to things that helped put everyone around him at ease.

I liked working with him and did so whenever given the opportunity.

———···———

After completing the arresting-officer paperwork on two of Tuhont County's Saturday night regulars, Jessie and Queen Hayes, Taft walked by Eli and used his clipboard to pop one of the county's newest deputies on the knee.

"If you don't have anything better to do, why don't you come along and let's ride a while?"

Lashe didn't hesitate. In short order, both deputies were headed out of town to work the southwest section of the county, Quadrant #3.

The department's patrol pattern was simple. On the map, Tuhont County was almost square. Starting from the northeast section, the numbering moved to the west, then to the south, then to the east and back to the north (Quadrant #1, to Quadrant #2, to Quadrant #3; to Quadrant #4).

For radio communications, the cars weren't numbered, the officers were. The sheriff was 1661; his son, Chief Deputy Dan Simpson was 1662 and on down the line. The car number was determined by the officer to whom it had been assigned for a given shift.

Just south of town, Taft (1665) went 10-7, to grab a late-night meal at Pathmore's Cafe. He hadn't eaten since mid-afternoon. The arrest and subsequent disposition on the Hayes duo had taken longer than usual, because Jessie and his wife were drunker, louder and meaner than usual.

Taft dropped Queen off at the jail before taking Jessie by the hospital for a couple of stitches. Typically he would've put the couple in the same cell to sleep it off. But that evening, they'd come to blows and Jessie looked to have gotten the worst of it. It wasn't hard to understand; Queen was about twice his size. To help hold the yelling and cursing down, Taft even put them on different halls.

———··———

After listening to Tate talk about his
ordeal with Jessie and Queen Hayes, I
suggested he eat slowly and enjoy his
hamburger steak. He'd earned a quiet meal, and
you'd think he could get one just after
midnight on CR 2250 at Pathmore's 24-hour café.
But it wasn't to be. Both the quiet and the
meal were short-lived.

The squalling tires, crunching collision
and spinning lights sent Tate and I
scrambling out of the booth as the pickup
came to a stop only yards from the front
windows. The other car remained in the middle
of the road, crumpled up and steaming.

Taft and I jumped in the jam of
midnight-diners trying to get out the front
door. I don't know where they all came from.
When we came in, it didn't seem to me that
there were that many occupied booths.

By the time we got to the road, Buford Willet was already pulling the driver out of the Camaro. Willet's buddy, a thug named Homer Gaddis, was clearly favoring a leg as he helped Buford drag the dazed driver out of the seat onto the pavement. They began to beat and kick the man in the stomach and head.

Tate went after Gaddis and I grabbed Willet. Gaddis was a bad customer, known for carrying a knife. But Tate quickly got him under control, using Mace, something our department had just gotten from the Smith & Wesson people. We'd been carrying it for only about a week.

Tate and I had our hands full, particularly me. Buford Willet, like his father and older brothers was a widely-known hooligan and self-proclaimed tough guy. As they say nowadays, he didn't just talk the talk, he walked the walk.

In his early-thirties, he'd already been charged with several assaults, one involving a deadly weapon. He'd spent time in the Tuhont County Jail for a variety of offenses and a state prison farm once.

Buford was long and stringy. I can still remember how strong, how powerful he was. I worked at staying in shape in those days, but when we went to the ground for the second time, the jury was very much out on whether I could handle Buford Willet.

I was not in uniform, had no Mace, no Billy Club or Slapjack. I did have a snub nose .38 in a belt holster under my jacket, handcuffs in a holster above my left hip and my badge in a leather sheath to the left side of my belt buckle.

At some point Willet managed to get my badge and start hitting me in the face with the deeply-embossed side. It hurt and bled like the dickens.

Things didn't move in my direction until I realized he had discovered my revolver and was trying to get the .38 out of the holster. That's when I was able to, as that television chef says - kick it up a notch or two. I had no doubt, if he succeeded in getting my gun, he would shoot me dead right there in the street. To be completely honest, that's exactly what he was whispering near my ear.

I don't know what to say when it comes to near-misses like that, and I hear people talking about your life flashing before your eyes. All I can say for sure is that I was fighting like hell, driven by fear and desperation. Movie star heroics are just that, something for the movies.

It seemed like a long time, but it was only a matter of moments before Tate Taft arrived and we managed to get Willet under control. Toward the end, two or three men that had been in the café jumped in to help.

I'll level with you. I delivered several extra blows before and during our efforts at subduing and getting Willet into the car.

There were very few times when I lost control with a subject like that. But I was still furious, very frightened and convinced Buford Willet meant to kill me if he could get control of that pistol. Him calling me every name in the book didn't help me gear down either.

Someone in the restaurant called for help shortly after things began. Two more of our cars and a state trooper unit arrived in fairly short order. With Willet and Gaddis cuffed in Tate's cruiser we were able to determine what happened.

Willet turned left into the café parking lot right in front of the southbound Camaro, which hit the pickup in the right rear tire, spinning it in a circle to the left. That's all it took to send Buford Willet into one of the rages for which his family was so famous.

On the way back to the jail, we swung by the hospital emergency room where they cleaned up scratches and abrasions on Willet and I. Gaddis' leg was examined and the injury was deemed a deep bruise.

——————··——————

After putting the two men in cells, both deputies went to the canteen for a cup of coffee and an opportunity for Tate Taft to continue his backgrounder on the Willets.

"I don't know, Eli, if there was ever an argument for some people being just born bad it might be the Emmett Willet clan. We've dealt with them for years. For a good while I thought the old man was about as bad as you could get. But his twin sons, Ben and Buck, have more than carried on the family tradition," said Taft, pausing to blow softly across his black coffee.

"Several years back there was trouble between the Willets and the Taylor family up in Polumbo County. I don't even remember what started it, probably nothin' much at all. But, it's never taken much to set the Willets off."

"The oldest Taylor boy disappeared after taking his girlfriend home one Friday night. His motorcycle was never found and it's the same with his body. I don't think there's the slightest doubt the Willet twins killed him, but no agency has been able to prove it. Ben's live-in girlfriend swears Ben and Buck were with her when Taylor disappeared."

Lashe wasn't all that familiar with the Willet's history, but he knew it was an appalling tale.

"Tate, what was it about the twin's mother?"

"Well, that's another sparkling piece of the Willet story."

"What was her name, now? Oh, yeah, Vera, Vera Willet. She simply disappeared about three years ago...just vanished."

"Word was she could drink Emmett under the table. Vera Willet was no prize, to be sure, but the investigation into her disappearance shouldn't have been allowed to lose steam. No family member, neighbor or friend kept pushing except an ailing sister who lives somewhere in Wisconsin. Emmett and the boys say she just up and moved out one day. Her husband and sons never even filed a missing persons report."

[65]

Eli stared at Taft for a few seconds. "And…what do you think happened, Tate?"

"I think she got drunk and raised hell with old man Willett one time too many."

———··———

It was around 2:30 in the morning and Tate had been gone about 10 minutes when I headed for the front door. The full time jailer, Chauncey Cobb, and Avery Cooley were in the back somewhere. My raw elbows were hurting, as well as my nicked-up face. A hot shower, the empty, quiet house and a soft bed had begun to sound very good.

Buck Willet was the first to explode into the lobby, knocking me to the floor with the right side of the heavy glass door. The next thing I knew, he was all over me, holding my ears and slamming my head into the linoleum floor. For the second time that night, I was fighting with one of the Willets, likely for my life.

It's always been a curiosity to me that in the second go-round, the thing I remember most about Buck's attack was the rank smell of his breath, liquor and all, as he breathed only inches from my face.

Then, all of a sudden, Buck was gone and Emmett Willet took over the attack. The old man had jerked his son out of the way and taken his place straddling my chest.

———··———

"Son of a bitch, beat on my boy and I'll kill ya!" shouted Emmett Willet as he moved from the deputy's head to his throat.

Eli was close to losing consciousness when he got to his revolver. Managing to resist an impulse to put one or more bullets through Emmett Willet, Lashe used the Smith & Wesson to land blows against the left side of the old man's head. With the fourth lick, Willet rolled away, stopping against the bottom of a floor-to-ceiling glass partition, only feet from the deputy's left shoulder.

As Lashe was trying to get to his feet, Ben Willet came through the doors and knocked Eli down with the homemade club he always carried under the seat in his truck.

That's when the really bizarre stuff started.

[67]

Both twins took an arm and began dragging Lashe out the door toward their pickup. They intended to haul him away from the jail and finish what they'd come to do – avenge the reported beating and un-warranted arrest of their little brother.

Someone who'd been at Pathmore's Café when it all happened told the Willets about the man in the yellow shirt who'd helped the deputy hit Buford several times before putting him in the sheriff's car. Three bad tempers and far too much Saturday night liquor brought the Willets to the Tuhont County Jail looking for blood.

Only feet from the pickup, Lashe's head cleared enough to understand what was going go, and he had no intentions of being taken anywhere. He pulled loose from Buck Willet and went after Ben. Without doubt, Bennett Willet had never been hit harder. He heard that crack and saw the flash that comes when someone hits you really hard, squarely in the mouth.

Chauncey Cobb and Avery Cooley got to the reception area about the same time. Cobb knelt to put cuffs on Emmett, while Avery Cooley went through the doors ready for the first Willet he saw. It was Buck.

———— ·· ————

I'd managed to get behind Ben and pull him backwards. There was nothing specialized about my actions; it wasn't some technique I'd learned in training; it was a plain old choke

[68]

hold, something I intended to continue until Ben Willet stopped resisting - hopefully in the short term and not for good.

Cooley hit Buck squared up, chest to back. The big, burly deputy locked his hands around Willet's chest, pinned Buck's arms by his sides, and started a violent side-to-side whipping action that took the largest of the twins a good 12-inches off the ground.

I think it's safe to say both Willets went limp about the same time. I don't remember exactly, but I'm pretty sure I turned loose of Ben before Avery turned loose of Buck. Avery Cooley looked and sounded like a grizzly bear taking it to Buck Willett. Thank goodness he got out there when he did. If he hadn't, Buck Willet would have likely gotten back to that club they liked to swing, and I would have left that street under a sheet.

It was well after dawn before things returned to anything resembling normal around the Tuhont County Courthouse. When the sun came up emotions were still high.

The Willets braved our turf in the most shocking of ways; they came right into the office, right into the place where officers feel most safe, looking for anyone. They ended up finding me, the man in the yellow shirt, and thankfully more than they expected in Avery Cooley.

I later learned Avery suffered from Tinnitus. His doctor told someone in the office he'd never treated anyone with a more severe case than Avery. I probably wouldn't feel like being chipper either if ringing or roaring in my ears was intense and constant.

As I wrote earlier, Avery and I grew a lot closer after taking on the Willets in the wee hours of the morning. Perhaps it was just a man thing, but something like a brothers-in-arms developed between us.

I don't believe he wanted many folks to know about his condition. But Avery smiled broadly when I winked and told him he wasn't the only one with ringing ears after the head-banging I endured in the Willet Wars.

DISPOSITION

Avery Cooley continued with the sheriff's department long after I'd left for the state, working for Dan after his father retired. The last I heard he'd moved back to his home state of West Virginia. I don't know why he left Tuhont County - just ready to go back home I guess.

Shortly after I joined the state patrol, Tate Taft accepted the chief position with a police department in south Florida. He and Betty only had one child - a daughter they nicknamed "Kitten". A disease took her hearing at an early age. It didn't take the bright child long to master lip reading. Even with that challenge, she was an exceptional student. After I'd gone to work with the Georgia State Patrol Dan Simpson told me her academics only grew more impressive. She went to a top school on scholarship and ended up working in research and product development for a major electronics company. (She wasn't in the 'Willet Wars' but it's something nice to know, don't you think?).

Emmett Willet fell over dead at a table in the jail common area during the court proceedings later that year. Looking at him in court, I thought he epitomized a leathered-looking old man who'd lived too rough and too reckless for too long.

The twins, Ben and Buck, faced and lost on a healthy list of charges. Both went to the penitentiary with long sentences handed down by Judge Rudolph "Rudy" Ayers. He'd prosecuted and presided over too many court sessions involving the Willets. They had fully confirmed their status as habitual offenders.

I don't remember how long it was both would be locked up. But I do remember thinking I'd probably be retired before the Willet twins would be on the street again.

The defense was successful in making a big deal out of Buford Willet defending himself against an officer "not in uniform". The question they hammered on was something like - how was he to know he was resisting a law enforcement officer, there was no uniform?

The fact he was hitting me in the face with my badge didn't seem to carry much weight. He got off light. I do know the man driving the Camaro brought suit against Willet and Gaddis for assault. Don't believe I ever heard how that came out.

The hard lick Ben Willet delivered with that oak club badly bruised my left shoulder and broke my collar bone. The broken clavicle, along with the dislocated thumb on my left hand slowed me down for a number of months.

But worst of all was the tear in the skin over the middle knuckle on my right hand and the cracked bone it exposed. Ben Willet's front teeth were responsible for both. Since that night, I've not been able to fully open my hand - not without some discomfort.

MY ONE AND ONLY MOONSHINE RAID
August 21, 1964

The sure-enough glory days of moonshine and moonshiners were pretty much over before I got into county law enforcement. In 1963, the year I became a deputy, Sheriff Simpson's department raided only three stills.

In 1964, the pace picked up some, particularly with one raid that took place at the foot of Perty's Peak - more on that to follow.

The three '63 stills were small, 5-to-8 gallon operations, and the third a little larger, set up in a barn on the back side of Casper Collins' property. Casper was a former county commissioner and lover of quality home squeezins.

Most of what I know about making, selling and distributing illicit whiskey I learned from Quentin "Sniffer" Blalock. He chased bootleggers in the Blue Ridge and Appalachian Mountains for well over 30 years, catching more than his share of operators and putting the fear of God into most of those who managed narrow escapes.

I first met Sniffer when I was still in the newspaper business. Our editor knew the long-time revenuer and thought he would be a key interview for our young feature-writer, Ken Shockley. Ken was doing a story on the culture of white liquor and the people who made it. Ken asked me to sit in.

———··———

Quentin suggested the two reporters come to his place, a rambling, restored, farm house that sat on fifteen acres in Polumbo County, 5-miles north of the Tuhont County line. The meeting took place on a large screened-in porch at 2:00 o'clock on a Sunday afternoon.

Blalock didn't look, act or talk like Shockley and Lashe expected. He was dark complected, had silver, almost shoulder-length hair; a scar that ran from just under the patch over his left eye to the corner of his mouth; a strikingly deep operatic voice and a large semiprecious stone in a heavy, yellow-gold mount on his right hand. That day he was wearing khaki slacks, sandals, and a light blue camp shirt, with a large tropical-flower print.

His words were more formal, more precise than might be expected from someone who'd traipsed through the woods cutting up stills going on four decades.

Lashe had been with the sheriff's department for several years before he learned Quentin Blalock taught high school literature before getting into the revenue side of law enforcement.

"We want to thank you for meeting with us today Mr. Blalock and helping with the story," said the young feature writer as he pulled the ladder-back chair closer to the round table.

"Certainly, but I'd like to get one thing straight right off. You guys please call me Sniffer. That's about all I answer to."

Shockley and Lashe smiled their willingness to do so. Both were anxious to get about the business of talking moonshine and hearing Blalock's insights on the subject. They knew he'd seen it all.

What made his perspective unique were his boyhood years, when he worked for his father at the family still and later made delivery runs into Atlanta and Knoxville. One way or another, Sniffer Blalock had been in the illegal liquor business all his life.

Shockley's first question was obvious. "How did you come by the name, 'Sniffer'?"

"Well, I've always been able to get out of the car at the head of some valley or along a ridge line and smell a still a mile away. The fact is, when the wind's right, I've smelled 'em from farther away than that. Today they use airplanes, but in the beginning my nose was all I needed."

Lashe and Shockley couldn't avoid laughing.

"Do you still use your nose?" asked Eli, fully expecting the answer he got.

"Sure I do. I just need to be a bit closer and have the wind a bit truer than I used to. If you'd ever smelled a really ripe operation, you'd discover it isn't all that hard to do."

"I understand you're quite a student of moonshine's history in the southeast. Could you tell us how things came about?"

"Well, Ken, that's quite a story, with about as many twists and turns as that creek down at the foot of the hill. And the story starts as far back as the creek's head waters up there on Bald Top Mountain. I'm not sure just how much detail you might want to hear...you interested in the long or short version?"

"Whatever you'd like to tell us would be fine."

Blalock grinned, sat back in his favorite rocker and began to summarize the history of illicit liquor in the southeastern United States, no small undertaking.

[78]

He began a backgrounder speaking of the Indian tribes which made liquor from native plants long before they had contact with English settlers. He moved on to talk about the pilgrims, who arrived with their own taste for homemade spirits and the skills to make them. Then Sniffer's account turned to England where the King began to levy taxes on the colonist's alcohol and other products. According to Blalock, that's when the settler's grumbling turned into gunfire.

Quentin paused in the narrative to pose a question. "Either one of you guys know that George Washington and Thomas Jefferson both operated large, private stills?"

"Back in the days of our founding fathers, it was the way to go."

Lashe and Shockley shook their heads, both enamored with Blalock's account.

Sniffer went on to point out that the anger and rebellious feelings toward England among still operators and small farmers were soon directed toward the new U.S. government, as it started taxing liquor (and tobacco) to pay off Revolutionary War debt.

"So, the struggle between moonshiners and revenuers goes way, way back?" asked Lashe.

Sniffer Blalock smiled and nodded as he answered. "Sure, right to the very beginning. Liquor was taxed back in the 15th century in Europe. And even back then it spurred illegal distilling operations."

"Where did the name 'moonshine' come from?" asked Shockley as he turned to a fresh page in his notebook.

"That goes back to Europe also, primarily England, where it referred to work that was done in the dark, illegal activity mostly. The word came over with the pilgrims and soon took root in America. And the word, 'bootlegger', is not nearly as old. It originated during colonial times when settlers would slip bottles of shine in their boots when smuggling product to the Indians."

The questions and answers soon confirmed the notion that producing illegal liquor was nothing new to rural southern Americans. In fact, it was basic to the culture, and over many decades the only skill many had to make a living.

"In the early days, we didn't just have the moonshiners against us. Making shine meant buying things like yeast, sugar and Mason jar supplies, all of which meant business for retailers, many of whom were prominent community leaders and elected officials.

Before the questions turned to the specifics of revenuer life, Sniffer's wife, Patty Anne, brought out a pitcher of lemonade. Ken and Eli were delighted with the opportunity to meet the lady Sniffer married when he was seventeen. Patty Anne was sixteen and working periodically at the Blalock family still.

With the pitcher half empty, the questions resumed.

"Sniffer, what was it like to track down and cut up a still in your earliest days as a revenuer?" asked Eli, already intrigued with a future involved in the cat-and-mouse of violators and law officers.

"Now, I don't want you to picture me in old-timey overalls, a straw in my mouth, a musket over my shoulder, and a large, tin star on my chest. I don't go back that far."

"But when I first started revenuing, things were pretty simple. It wasn't unusual to bust up fifteen to twenty stills a month in some of these mountain counties, particularly if you didn't care all that much about catching the operators. If chopping one up was all you wanted to do, you could come through the woods like an Army battalion and have at it. Catching folks in the act called for a focus on quality, not just quantity."

"In the thirties and forties stills were what most people picture when you talk about them today – well back in the woods, rough and ready in every way. Many moonshiners were armed and their hounds were trained to sound the alarm if someone was headed in their direction. Some distillers reacted violently when we showed up, not all, but some. It was dangerous business, and we took it seriously. If they're smart, today's officers will exercise just as much caution as we did back then."

"I remember raiding a still back in '49. It was in the extreme western corner of North Carolina – way back in the boonies. I mean way back. It was about thirty

[81]

minutes before dawn and we were within a hundred yards of the cooker when a crack split the air."

"Agent Roy Steele never knew what hit him. The slug went in on the right side at the base of his neck and came out through his left kidney. That's what happens when the shot is taken from thirty feet up an oak tree. It stopped us all in our tracks, and every one of those scoundrels got away but the guy in the tree. We shot him dead before he got his first foot on the ground."

Blalock paused a moment, looking off toward Bald Top and the blue-gray mountains beyond. Then he expressed his thought; "Ambush! That's what I always feared the most."

"Back then there were always more of them than us. Hell, I've seen the days when there were only eight or ten agents to work an entire state. If it hadn't been for local support, we'd never had gotten the job done. And then, of course, the more people who knew about a planned raid, the more likely the operators were to hear about it. Back then, when it came to moonshine, you weren't always sure how to separate the good guys from the bad."

Ken Shockley asked the next question.

"How'd you guys get around? What kind of cars did the agencies provide?"

Blalock smiled broadly and seemed to drift off again, perhaps dwelling on thoughts he hadn't pulled up in years. "Oh, Ken, there were no agency cars; no flashing lights or fancy pistol and hardware belts; no high-powered hand guns; only drab .38 revolvers and a sawed-off, double-barrel shotgun, both of which I provided. The majority of the time working the backroads I drove my own car, first a Ford and then a Chevy. My uniform was coveralls and brogans. On most of the raids I carried the .38 in my front pocket – along with a rabbit's foot my dad gave me."

"Years back the state did install two-way radios in our vehicles, which permitted ATF folks to communicate with state and some county officers. Before they did that, it could get mighty lonely in the wee hours of the morning riding alone on some two-lane dirt road way back the foothills."

Eli picked up on the image of a lone revenuer working a rural highway in the dark, looking for liquor cars. "I know all your time wasn't spent in the woods. You also worked the roads. What was that like?"

"Well, the stories people have heard about souped-up liquor cars are probably more true than false. Some of the cars they drove would really fly, and they knew how to drive them. In addition to having a lot of power, the really slick operators installed rear end pumps to off-load either liquor or motor oil on the highway. They could choose between dumping the evidence and trying to spin out their pursuers."

"When you saw headlights coming through the woods on a single-lane, dirt road at 3:00 o'clock in the morning, you could count on two things: it wasn't vacationers and the bootlegger was already trying to turn around."

"There was one guy in particular, Skinny Smallwood, who could drive a car better backwards than I could straight ahead. He did it twice that I'm sure of. Once he got to the pavement, he'd simply hammer down and outrun me. My Ford and Chevy were both stout. On the straight and level they'd motor. But I can't tell you how many times I couldn't even keep Skinny's taillights in sight."

———— ··· ————

When I think back on it, seems like the first half of the interview focused on facts and figures; and as you might expect, the second half was filled with stories about the good old days and the good old boys.

It wasn't until Sniffer was walking us back to the car that we felt comfortable enough to ask about the silky, black patch. He said it would please him greatly to tell us he'd lost the eye overpowering a big, hard-muscled bootlegger, but he couldn't do that. It seems he didn't see the snarl of barbed wire as he was chasing an operator through the woods somewhere near the Alabama-Georgia state line. I'll do for you what I wish Sniffer had done for us - spare you the grisly details.

Three hours after the interview began we were headed back to Asheford. It had been very informative and very fascinating.

I've often thought the three hours on Sniffer's back porch was one of the most influential experiences in furthering my interest in law enforcement as a career. What really impressed me was the smile on his face as he described experiences, successes and more than a few failures doing what he wanted to do most.

In the mid-sixties raids on stills described by Quentin Blalock had fallen from monthly highs of 20 to 25 to only 3 or 4. But that didn't mean there was less moonshine on the market. In fact, one out of every 5 gallons of liquor in the country was illegally-made when I worked for Tuhont County, a full 20%. While the number of stills in the 50's and 60's went down, the capacity of larger, more sophisticated equipment and methods went up - fewer stills producing more shine.

There was no was no better example of a higher-capacity operation than the still run by Otto Kearns and his younger brother, Leon. The Kearns family had made hooch for decades, and gotten away with it. Their father, Percy, was one of the originals, known for some of the best white liquor around.

According to Sheriff Simpson, Percy Kearns used to say the old stories about automobile radiators used in the distilling process and throwing dead animals in the mash to quicken fermentation was "hogwash, pure hogwash!" The sheriff said Percy argued white liquor was smoother, better-tasting and better for you than store-bought booze. If there was such a thing, the Kearns family was one of Georgia's quality moonshine clans.

We gathered at the sheriff's office a couple of hours before dawn on Friday August 21, 1964. Sheriff Simpson, Chief Deputy Dan Simpson, Deputies Tate Taft, Howard Bone and I, along with ATF agents Bill Smart, Quentin Blalock and Ben Lacy were preparing to head for Acorn Ridge, the general stomping grounds of the Kearns family.

Three weeks earlier one of the ATF guys noticed two head-high spruce trees on Acorn Ridge Road leaning slightly in different directions. He looked closer and found they'd been stuck in the ground - a favorite trick to help conceal a path leading back into the woods. That coupled with a flyover helped locate the latest Kearns operation.

It was hidden on the upper end of Clear Sap Creek. The Kearns were well-connected in the city and they took their work as seriously as they did the heavy-duty cash it pulled in from suburban Atlanta. Everyone in the meeting understood things could go badly, if the Kearns family wanted them to. Even the most experienced in the group knew slipping up on Otto and Leon Kearns, as well as the renegade help they attracted would come with risks.

———··———

Sheriff Simpson made a few remarks before the small caravan left for Acorn Ridge.

"Okay, guys, the still is located up in a draw. The hillsides are right steep on both sides. Pretty much the only way to get in there without making all kinds of noise slidin' down the slopes is to go in head-first. We'll have to take that as it comes. One of the guys the Kearns brothers stiffed out of $200 gave us a call and said both Otto and Leon were supposed to be there."

"Everyone here is familiar with the Kearns brothers and most of us have dealt with them in one way or another. They're tough ol' boys, especially Leon, and we're gonna need to have our wits about us."

"We've already gone over who will team up and how we'll spread out heading up the draw. It's likely there'll be weapons on site, particularly if Otto and Leon are working."

Around 4:30 AM three vehicles, one a county prisoner transfer van, pulled out of the Tuhont County courthouse parking lot and headed north toward Acorn Ridge.

It would prove a morning none of the eight officers would forget.

———··———

Our group was larger than the number of officers usually taking part in a liquor raid. Of course the Kearns operation was a larger-than-average prize. We didn't know how many we might find at the still, but from the information we had it was likely to be 5 to 7, counting Otto and Leon. None of us were kidding ourselves about being able to round up everyone there.

When we went over the sketch Sheriff Simpson had drawn, showing the final approach to the still itself, few of us believed things would hold together as

[89]

planned. They hardly ever did. The trick was to synchronize the final few yards so we could come at them from several directions at the same time.

When we got into the woods and started up the draw, we found it narrower than expected. The steeper sides forced what were originally 4 teams of 2-men-each, into 2 teams of 4-men-each.

I don't remember anyone at that time saying anything about that situation, but I can tell you, none of us liked being bunched up like that. We looked and felt like those fish-in-a-barrel you've heard about.

We were within 50-yards of the still proper when it broke loose.

A handgun went off first, followed by a medium-gauge rifle. One of the two took off the lower half of Ben Lacy's right ear. He was in the other group of four, toward which most of the ambush was directed - thank God.

Before that Friday morning in August of '64 the only place I'd used my service revolver was at the firing range. It certainly hadn't been enough to prepare me for a sudden, heavy exchange of gunfire. I don't want to say our effort went to mush. But the two groups of four instantly became 8 singles. I'll confess, for the next 5 to 10 minutes, I did as much crouching, tree-hugging and hiding as I did aiming and shooting.

Most of the firing sounded much more erratic than target-specific. I remember seeing and getting off a shot at some guy running up the valley in front of us. After sunrise we found I'd missed the bootlegger but I got his dog - not my intention, I assure you.

During what I think can reasonably be called a good, old-fashioned shootout, one thing I remember clearly is the sporadic, pops and cracks of the small-caliber gunfire set against shouts drifting down that valley. I think about it every time I hear a shoot 'em up sound track in an old movie on TV.

When it seemed like the ambushers had headed in the other direction, I found myself running alongside ATF Agent Bill Smart. There was only one worker nearby when we broke into the still clearing - Roscoe Combs.

Roscoe, who had a deformed right leg, was hiding behind a large stump. He twice ignored Smart's order to get on his feet. When Billy grabbed him by the back of the collar to pull him up, Combs came up spinning to his left.

The heavy, glass jug he swung in his right hand hit Bill Smart in the face. It was bad, very bad!

Combs, who was a well-known, freelance bootlegger in his own right, gave it his best

trying to run up the hill. He didn't get far
before I caught up and got him on the ground.

He may have had a bum leg, but there
was nothing wrong from the waist up.

At times I could have sworn there was
two of him. The old codger didn't stop fighting
until I got the barrel of my revolver in his
mouth and made it absolutely clear I would
pull the trigger. At that moment, I was afraid
of having to do just that.

Roscoe only had a tooth here and there,
but what was there left a painful bite on my
arm. The look of those teeth and the thought
of them sunk into my forearm has always
bothered me. Sometimes, thinking about
something completely unrelated, I'll catch
myself rubbing the two scars near my left
elbow.

It was well after dawn before we could
determine what we'd done and failed to do -

two arrests (several others missed), four pickaxes worth of destruction on elaborate cooking and distilling equipment, 50-gallons of white liquor poured out and one 58-model Dodge pickup impounded.

I helped cut up several other stills in my time with Tuhont County, and one while with the Georgia State Patrol. But the only true raid I ever helped conduct featured an ambush, a gunfight, and a painful encounter with a snaggletoothed bootlegger.

DISPOSITION

Running down a man on the Kearns raid, Quentin Blalock suffered a badly broken right ankle. He managed to hold on to the guy until some help arrived. But the painful break in the woods near Perty's Peak and the nasty loss of his left eye to barbed wire in another moonshiner chase, proved enough to end Sniffer's career. He retired in 1969 and died on his Polumbo County farm about 10 years later.

Both Kearns brothers were in fact at the still that night, but both made good their escape. I'm afraid I can't tell you much about either of them. I know Leon got in trouble on non-liquor-related charges in Atlanta, receiving stolen goods or something like that.

Otto seemed to just disappear. He was seen a time or two after the raid, but that was it. His wife had died shortly before their still was destroyed. That, coupled with the loss of their latest and greatest enterprise, may have simply been enough to send him into retirement in a different neck of the woods.

Roscoe Combs was brought up on several charges. He was a pitiful ol' character, slow of foot and mind, and I felt like the judge took that into consideration. He was given a fairly light sentence at a nearby state prison farm. He died less than a year later.

After his death, I was kidded for quite a while about Roscoe dying from food poisoning. That may have been the case, if adrenalin can cause it.

His colleagues said they never heard Ben Lacy complain about the missing earlobe. He must have been fully aware of the good fortune that was his as the bullet whizzed by, barely missing his face.

There were several dental and surgical procedures performed on Billy Smart. I made a note in my diary back then - broken nose, broken teeth and dislocated jaw. He too might have been lucky to be alive. It turned out to be only slightly worse than it looked, and it did look awful, with his bloody, broken lower teeth sitting about an inch to the right of his uppers.

Speaking of lucky, I can remember thinking Roscoe Combs had some good fortune that night as well. As Bill Smart was falling backwards he fired his pistol from about the right hip. The bullet couldn't have missed Combs head by more than a few inches.

One other note here - that Dodge pickup was sold at auction. There was some satisfaction in watching two members of the Kearns family buy back their own vehicle.

A CROOK AMONG CRIMINALS
August, 1965

In the late summer of 1965, we'd been looking for Bernard Gohagan almost a year, looking hard for the biggest little shyster to ever come out of Cedar Row.

Every form of bulletin and interagency communication was used to get out the word on the community's controller-turned-crook.

Cedar Row had one red light, seven or eight store-front buildings, a handful of stop signs, two police officers (one full and one part-time), one police car, one well-seasoned fire engine, and a budget big enough to arouse the unprincipled interests of Bernard Lewis Gohagan.

Over the course of two-plus years, he managed to embezzle quite a bit of money. I don't remember the exact amount, but I recall it being more than a few thousand dollars.

Gohagan lived by himself in a small duplex apartment, and for the most part stayed at home, except when at the city office. He'd never married, and was pretty much helpless without his thick glasses and Zenith hearing aids. There was little imposing about the 5' 5", balding, 50-year-old, mostly self-taught accountant.

What was really impressive, were the deceptive paper trails he devised to cover up the tax and grant dollars he'd siphoned off the city's cash flow, along with the way he managed to avoid capture. But his time on-the-lam came to an end when we got a call from Detroit telling us that Gohagan was in jail up there.

It was a call that redirected the next 6 days of my life.

———···———

Lashe was walking by Earl Simpson's door when the sheriff hung up the phone and called the three-year deputy into his office.

"Eli, I just got off the phone with authorities in Detroit. Bernard Gohagan is in the Cook County Jail. They picked him up on a DUI charge a couple of weeks back and finally got around to running a check on him."

"Detroit? How'd Gohagan get way up there? Folks in Cedar Row weren't sure he even had a car when he skipped town."

"Well, that's somethin' you can ask him yourself....when you pick him up."

Eli paused, his bottom jaw dropping slightly.

"You mean you want me to go up there and bring him back?

"Yes I do, but I don't want you to go alone. I want you to call Buster Maxey in Cedar Row and see whether him or that part time officer is gonna go with you."

"Sheriff, now you know he'll send Barnes. Buster Maxey's not goin' away from home that long. Sheriff, come on, ridin' all the way up to Detroit and back with Arlen Barnes...?"

"Oh, Eli, it won't be too bad. Coming back it'll be a threesome – you, Barnes and ol' Bernie," replied Sheriff Simpson with a slightly mocking smile.

———··———

I couldn't hardly type this out without

a picture of Arlen Barnes in my mind and a

[101]

smile on my face. What at character! He was just over 5-feet tall, always scruffy looking, a chain smoker, and paunchy enough to pull gaps between the bottom 2-or-3 buttons on his uniform shirt. He's the first person I remember wearing a baseball style (police) hat cocked to the right about 20 degrees. I know that's popular with many young folks today, but back then it called for a double-take.

But what got to me most, thinking about the long trip ahead, was his endless chatter. Everybody knew Arlen was a talker, with a real talent when it came to emphasizing the obvious.

I was right. Buster Maxey sent Arlen Barnes.

But I've got to eat a little crow here. There were a few rough spots, but to my pleasant surprise, the ride up to Michigan wasn't as bad as I'd feared. As it turned out, he slept most of the time, on two or three occasions, stretched out in the back seat.

The '60 Ford we were in was the oldest unit we had on the road in 1965. There are several things I remember about that Fairlane 500 - its under-dash air conditioning unit; the complete absence of any police markings; the smallest rear-deck antenna I'd ever seen; and the two big, flattened-out fins on the back. The only emergency light we used with it was a small, magnetic red spinner we shuffled on and off the roof above the driver's door.

There are a couple of things on the ride up I might mention. First, the A/C quit shortly after we left for Detroit. Barnes and I didn't realize just how much the small box helped until we lost it, in the middle of August.

The other had to do with some early-morning atmospherics.

About 7:30 we'd finished breakfast and gotten in the car to head over to the Cook County Jail, when Arlen reached forward and got the mic. Jokingly he announced, I'm gonna report in. "1667 to Tuhont County, we're 10-8".

The reply shocked us both, "10-4, 1667".

Needless to say, both of us snapped to some form of attention and spun our heads in one another's direction. We were laughing when, whoever it was, came back to us again. "1667, I thought you were in Detroit".

We told them we were. The radio skip lasted a couple of minutes, us sitting on the edge of downtown Detroit talking to the folks at home. Over 700 miles from the Tuhont County Jail and that small antenna reached out to the base unit back in Asheford. I never had it happen but that one time.

Pulling into one of the parking lots at the Cook County Department of Corrections was quite an experience for two guys who were used to taking one of the 25 parking spaces in the single lot just outside the Tuhont County Jail. Our eye-popping reaction only grew stronger when we walked into the reception area.

———— ·.· ————

Lashe took the lead entering what looked to be the first of three cellblock buildings. Arlen Barnes walked just behind.

Both Lashe and Barnes were struck by the noticeable, echo-like drone coming from the highly-polished hallways running in several directions, people crisscrossing right and left.

Comment: Although he didn't include it here, Eli told me he picked up a shoe-polishing kit the night before and got Arlen to work at putting a fresh coat of polish on the brown shoes he always wore with the black uniform pants. Eli also succeeded in putting a shine on Arlen's gunbelt and badge. As Eli expected, Barnes wore (and slept in) his only uniform. Eli was in civvies.

"What can I do for you two?" asked one of the two officers working the front desk. Their dead-pan look served to confirm the wearisome routines involved in dealing with a thousand inmates and their families on a daily basis. A busy month put no more than fifteen to twenty in our place back home.

[105]

"Yes. I'm Deputy Eli Lashe with the Tuhont County Georgia Sheriff's Department, and this is officer Arlen Barnes with the Cedar Row PD. We're here to pick up Bernard Lewis Gohagan" said Lashe, showing his badge, along with Sheriff Simpson's letter of introduction, and other legal documentation authorizing Gohagan's release into his deputy's custody.

With no further acknowledgement, the Cook County officer picked up the phone, spun in his chair, almost fully turning his back to Lashe, and spoke softly into the receiver. When he "returned", his directions were simple: "Have a seat over there and someone will come to get you." He pointed to a row of metal chairs against a far wall where ten to fifteen people were already seated.

The 'someone' that walked in from a hallway on the far side was a petite, twenty-something-year-old that said only, "Lashe?"

After four or five turns, passing offices, waiting rooms and one cluttered break area, the young female officer stopped, spun, and extended her hand toward a room where three uniformed men were seated.

The large, Hispanic-looking sergeant at the middle desk motioned Lashe and Barnes into the room. Before saying a word, he picked up the phone, pushed one of clear plastic buttons, waited a moment and said, "They're here. Go get him".

He'd no more than hung up the phone, than it buzzed loudly, prompting him to raise his right index finger in a just-a-moment gesture. Without the first word to Lashe and Barnes, he spoke his fifth into the phone, "Castro."

Comment: When Eli briefed me and asked I write this part of the story for him, he said remembering that officer's name had always been easy....for the obvious reason.

Following several moments listening to the person on the other end, Castro blurted out: "I don't care what the son-of-a-bitch has to say about it or how often he complains with the belly ache at meal time....he stays in solitary and tell him he's close to getting another couple of weeks added on."

Then he slammed down the handset before returning to the two Georgia officers.

"So, you two are here to pick up, Mr. Peepers?" – an obvious reference to the smallish Wally Cox who'd worn heavy, black-rimmed glasses in the television series of the same name in the 1950's.

That crack and the curtness they'd experienced since walking in the front door was getting to Eli.

"That's what we're here for if by, Mr. Peepers you mean Bernard Lewis Gohagan," replied Lashe, with a combination of added emphasis on and hesitation between each word serving to confirm growing irritation.

Even Arlen Barnes was able to overcome his apprehension long enough to exchange glances with Lashe and draw an immediate mental comparison between their uncongenial reception and the warm greeting they'd grown accustomed to when Sheriff Simpson received a visitor.

[107]

It was Castro's next question that really set things off. Sitting up in his squeaky, swivel chair and leaning across the paperwork on his desk, he inquired, without the slightest reservation.

"Tell me….uh….Deputy Lashe, you ever been to a lynching? I thought you might be able to tell me what that was like. I mean, we hear so much about that going on down where you come from."

Both Tuhont County men flexed, Eli noticeably more than Arlen.

"No, afraid not Castro.....what with all the squirrel huntin', high-boot plowin', wood splittin', rabbit skinnin', clod hoppin', wife-beatin', liquor makin' and shit kickin' I have to do, just don't seem like I've had the time. But, I tell you what, why don't you come on down one day and maybe we country cops can show you how we deal with an arrogant ass."

The quick and crafted reply caught Castro completely off guard. The men on his left and right returned to their paperwork, each trying but failing to rein in a laugh.

Before anything else was said, two officers escorted Bernard Gohagan into the room.

————··————

Arlen was even more shocked than I was when we first saw Gohagan. I remembered him as being small-framed. But the hollow-faced, gaunt individual that walked into the office looked terrible. We assumed his year on the run had taken a great deal out of him - at least that was our first thought.

Within 30 minutes we were back in the Fairlane heading out of Detroit. Both Barnes and I were watching Gohagan in the rearview mirrors. Before we left the building, he'd started shaking and didn't stop until we were quite a few miles down the road.

Nobody said much until we put some distance between ourselves and the jail. As we cleared the city proper, Arlen turned and asked Gohagan how he was feeling. That's when Bernie started to cry. Even today, I'm still not sure I've ever heard or seen anyone cry like that. He put his face in his cuffed hands and bent over on his knees. The tension he released and emotion he showed was incredible.

The crying became wailing, filled with thanks to God and to us for his "deliverance".

Arlen, who knew Geohagan far better than I, unfastened his seat belt, turned around and leaned over into the backseat, removed the cuffs and began trying to calm Gohagan down. During his first year as Cedar Row's controller, Bernard had been a friend to Arlen, introducing him to Buster Maxey and helping get him the part time job with the police department.

Not until we pulled into a roadside diner and went inside for coffee and a sandwich did Gohagan really calm down. I remember feeling something like a third wheel when he hugged Arlen for the second time after getting out of the car. For the next several minutes he couldn't talk about anything but how much he missed "the people back home" and how "blessed" he was that we'd come to get him.

Thirty minutes later we knew why he felt that way.

His time on the run hadn't really been all that bad. He'd stayed in a couple of men's shelters, found a cash-paying job at a carwash, and spent some time just traveling the back roads in a car he'd bought from a private seller.

His tough times, the days when pressure pulled him down so badly, had come in the past two or three weeks, and tough they were.

He talked about the killing that took place in the shower room, and the rape he listened to several cells down from his own.

More than anything else though, he talked about two prisoners and a guard who bullied and beat him. They stole and broke his glasses, while making fun of his hearing aids. One prisoner pulled them from his ears, shouting, "Zenith, I thought they only made TV's, little man!" Both inmates pushed them into their ears before tossing them into the toilet. Gohagan was able to retrieve only one.

The cracked lens in his glasses and the single hearing aid hanging down, more in front of his ear than in it, made him look even more exhausted and undone in that diner booth.

The two worst inmates he encountered beat him once with bars of soap slung in socks. What concern I might have had about exaggeration went away after he pulled up his shirt and showed us the terrible bruises on his stomach, back and sides.

I asked him why they treated him like that, and his answer was simple: "They said it was because I was from the South".

But it was what came next that really explained the tears and deep expressions of relief. He told us the man in the cell next to him whispered something frightening around the wall at the bars: "Mr. Peepers, they plannin' on killin' you tomorrow - just thought you oughta know".

That's when I remembered, we had in fact picked him up two days earlier than originally scheduled - the day before they planned to carry out their worst threat.

Watching in the rearview mirror as Mr. Peepers laid his head on the back of the seat and slept heading home, I had a thought that's never really left me - a thought I adopted when filtering my responses in all situations dealing with citizen offenders — there really is a difference in a crook and a hardened criminal.

DISPOSITION

Bernard Lewis Gohagan went to jail for his misdeeds, but I can't tell you where or for how long. I remember his sentence was greatly reduced after he returned the lion's share of the money he'd taken. Believe it or not, over time he'd turned it into cash and kept it in Crisco cans. He'd spent only a fraction - most of it on that car I believe.

Just months after our trip to Detroit, Arlen Barnes lost his job with the Cedar Row Police Department. I heard he went to work with the humane society. He loved animals, something he told me more than a few times on the way to Detroit.

"BIG ROWDY"
May 13, 1966

Deputy Howard Bone and I were eating the Friday special at Toni's Restaurant. There was nothing Italian about Toni Spearman, but she made some of the best red sauce ever. Every third Friday the daily special was lasagna and that day was one of the third Fridays. Good stuff!

Boney went to work with Sheriff Simpson in the late 50's, and had been a friend to me since my earliest days with the department. He always seemed interested in what you had to say - a good and patient listener. That day in May he was tasked with hearing-me-out as I described my morning troubles.

I started by telling him about our 17-month-old, Ernie, leaning to the side in his highchair and pulling a bowl off the kitchen table. Its contents went all over the walls and front of our recently-refinished kitchen cabinets.

It seemed like gravy found every nook and cranny in the room. I remember the clean-up put Millie and I in the floor on our hands and knees, as well as on the top rung of a stepladder used to reach the ceiling.

Pausing only while Jenna Goodson refilled our coffee cups, I continued my report by describing the stale scrambled eggs and hard biscuits following the time cleaning up and a third hug, which I hoped would further console my wife.

Boney was forced to listen as I went on to describe changing the cruiser's right rear tire in the soft-shoulder mud along a recently-widened part of Cherry Lane. I had been on the road only 5-minutes before the relatively-new tire flattened out.

From the beginning, Boney was trying to suppress laughter. But when half the coffee in my just-filled cup went down the front of my uniform he couldn't hold it any longer. It took a moment on my part, but we ended up sharing a real belly-laugh.

Comment: Eli didn't explain here, but he'd told me before that Howard Bone came by the nickname, "Boney", in two ways: a play on his last name and a reference to his build – about 6' 5" and 170 pounds.

When the laughter slowed Boney leaned across the table and said, "Well, Eli, after all, it is Friday the 13th." The way things began and ended that day, the second Friday in May, 1966, always pops in my mind when someone mentions the 13th and Friday in the same breath.

About 30-minutes after lunch, I was in the south-central part of the county working the Gilmore area when I received the call. It was unusual to get a 10-10 in the middle of the afternoon, but the day had featured the unexpected; why not a fight right after lunch, in broad daylight, in the middle of the road?

—————··—————

Renea Raney was working the radio desk.

"Tuhont County to 1667."

"Go ahead, Tuhont," replied Lashe, who'd just gotten back into the car after stopping for a soft drink.

"'67, what's your '20?"

"I'm at Witt's Grocery, just west of Gilmore Crossroads."

"Okay, we got a call from Todd's Child Care, 122 Jones Avenue, reporting a fight in progress. Fretta Todd said three men are fighting in the middle of the street. She advised one of the men involved is Harland Shoemaker."

"10-4, Tuhont, I'm on the way."

Things picked up when Lashe heard the name, Harland Shoemaker. Raney didn't need to elaborate. Lashe knew of at least two outstanding warrants on one of Tuhont County's roughest characters. Several agencies wanted him. Eli had been in on two previous attempts to corner Shoemaker, only to have him slip away each time.

"Tuhont County did the woman say she was sure it was Shoemaker?" asked Eli as he sped toward the southern end of Asheford.

"She advised there's no doubt one of them is him. She said he's a former neighbor and he's fighting right in front of the front window in her building."

Just as Lashe left Blackshear Road and merged onto the Quarry Highway, Raney came back with further word: "1667, I've notified Asheford PD and 1661 has just left here en route the scene. The city said their ETA was five to six minutes. There's also a state unit en route, GSP 7-05."

———···———

I remember thinking the city would likely get to Jones Avenue before I could. I really wanted to be part of taking down Harland Shoemaker, but as it turned out, other things would take precedence.

Quarry Highway was really more a wide, well-maintained county road than a true highway. It didn't carry a state or federal highway number. The old rock quarry had been shut down for years, but Quarry Road remained one of the main north-south traffic arteries through Tuhont County.

Muskrat Creek ran parallel to the road for several thousand feet south of Asheford. In places it broadened into what seemed more like a river than a creek, but for the most part it was about 10-feet wide and no more than 8 to 10 inches deep.

I must have been running 80 or better when I rounded the sweeping curve about 6 miles south of the city limits. The first thing that caught my attention was taillights and then the black skid marks trailing off the highway to the left toward the water.

The blue Dodge two-door was sitting on its top. As I braked to a stop, 50-plus yards past the Dart, I saw all four wheels were still spinning. It had just happened. A quick check down the road and in the rearview mirror confirmed that no traffic was approaching from either direction. I centered the cruiser in the middle of the road and began backing up as fast as I could.

Having the arrest of Harland Shoemaker on my mind and then running up on a vehicle lying on its top in a creek had my head spinning. Backing up as hard as I could, I almost went in Muskrat Creek myself. It took an effort and some luck to get the BelAir back under control. After the erratic backward weaving, I eased up on the throttle and managed to back over onto the shoulder about 20 to 30 feet from the Dodge.

I remember debating for an instant whether or not I should call in before getting out. I can't say I recall making a decision really; I just remember running in the slippery, wet grass toward the overturned car. That's when someone inside set down on the horn and began yelling.

———..———

The words were panicked, "Help me! God, please help me!"

The bank down from Quarry Highway to the creek was six or seven feet high at a 45-degree angle. Getting down to the creek, the Tuhont deputy did more sliding than walking.

The driver continued to cry for help: "Oh my God! Somebody get me out of here. There're killing me!" The driver's next shouts were drowned out by a second, long, blast on the horn and a wide-open revving of the engine which had continued to run.

———— ··· ————

Just as I reached the driver's door, I was knocked backwards by a large dog. It seemed to come from nowhere. I later determined the boxer scrambled out the passenger side window, across the underside of the car and straight over me, heading up the bank toward the pavement.

I got back to my feet, and again went down beside the open driver's side window. From what I could see, the male driver was the only person in the car.

The relatively shallow water didn't appear an immediate danger, but the swarming yellow jackets were. They were all over him. He'd obviously rolled over a large nest on the bank or at the edge of the creek. I was no expert on yellow jackets then nor am I today, but I knew swarming and attacking like they were could cost the man his life.

I pulled at the handle but was only able to open the door a few inches. The car was leaning in my direction and the top edge of the door hit the ground long before opening wide enough to get him out.

As I jerked on the handle the first two yellow jackets got me - one under my chin and the second on my left hand between the little and ring finger. Then came stings number three and four, both on my neck. I'm sure I was fully consumed by the task at hand, but I can still remember how badly the stings hurt. And

I can recall the flurry as they swarmed around us both. One got in my ear, and I'm here to testify that will distract you from any task at hand.

Just after I'd gotten the angry, yellow critter out of my ear, my growing fear and feeling of helplessness was broken. I didn't see him come running up, but I sure heard him when he got to the passenger door.

———— ... ————

Lashe was swatting at stinging insects and trying to communicate with the frantic driver, when the huge man came out of nowhere. Suddenly he was just there, towering over the other side of the Dodge Dart, shouting instructions to the deputy: "Get out of the way, man! Get out of the way! I'm gonna roll it over!"

Eli stood and looked across the underside of the car at the huge man in the tall, wide-brimmed cowboy hat. Lashe didn't argue, it seemed the thing to do at that moment was follow instructions; and he did, scrambling away from the overturned car.

The newcomer had assessed things coming down the hill and realized the car would roll easier toward rather than away from Quarry Highway. He bent low and placed the up-turned heel of both hands in the bottom of the open window. Once getting the car up far enough, he slipped his shoulder below the edge of the roof. From that point he spun and backed up, rolling the car over on its wheels.

———··———

I'd managed to call for help in the middle of things. Another of our units and an ambulance arrived shortly. The driver was covered in red splotches, more wet than dry, and bleeding from a nasty cut on his forehead. But, he was alive. Among his first words were, "Where's my dog?"

DISPOSITION

At some point between us getting the driver out of the car and into the ambulance, the big fellow slipped away. I never found out his name, but a trooper who'd responded said "Big Rowdy" was painted on the door of his rig. I don't recall the name of the guy driving the Dart. I do know he recovered from all those stings.

They insisted I go to the hospital. I did. No allergic reaction. That night Millie treated nearly two dozen stings with salve and pennies. Someone told her putting a penny on the sting helped - something about the copper. The day started with splattered gravy and flat tires. It ended with pennies strategically placed on my arms, neck and face. What a Friday the 13th!

I'm happy to report that Asheford PD was successful in arresting Harland Shoemaker.

"YOOOO HOOOO" YOU TWO

July, 1966

I've always loved a Yoo Hoo© chocolate
drink. You know, it's the one in the small
bottle with the yellow, blue and red label -
the one people can't figure out - is it milk, is
it a chocolate powder mix, or is it some kind
of non-carbonated, specialty-flavored cola?

As you probably know, you've gotta
shake 'em up, but after you do, they're great.
I've long since quit worrying about how
they're made. I just drink 'em.

Every day after high school football
practice I'd wait for my father to pick me up
at Agnew's Grocery. We seldom left without
several packs of peanut butter 'n cheese
crackers and at least two bottles of right-
out-of-the-ice Yoo Hoo© chocolate drink.

But, I've had a long-time problem when it
comes to drinking Yoo Hoo©. Perhaps "problem"

[127]

isn't the right word. Maybe "issue" would be better.

I can't screw off the top without thinking about a ride I took with Earl Simpson back in 1966.

I was working with the Sheriff late in the week of July 4th that year. One of our officers was out sick, and as I recall another had taken a week off to visit out-of-town family. Anyway, the Sheriff was filling in.

In his final years, he used one of the older Belvederes and toured the county by himself. He loved to monitor the radio and follow the action, arriving on scene just after the rough stuff had been put to rest. But throughout much of his career he would get out with a deputy and take a full patrol shift.

The 4th fell on a Monday, and the weekend had been very active. The jail was booked to capacity. Before we left the parking lot, Sheriff Simpson and I talked about the possibility of a quiet night with most of the Cain having been raised the weekend before.

It was around 6:30PM, and we were as to yet see our first speeder. There was one noisy-dog complaint, but resolving that squabble between two elderly neighbors required only a few smiles and Sheriff Simpson's gentlemanly approach to things.

The Sheriff was at the wheel and we were parked across from Vonda's Watering Hole on State Highway 112 south of Asheford.

It was a good spot to monitor two of the county's most-ignored stop signs several hundred feet down the road. Keeping an eye on the Cooper Road/Highway 112 intersection was time well spent. Policing the busy crossroads location was something every officer should have probably taken more seriously. The accident rate there was one of the highest in the county.

Of course, watching Vonda's customers walk (sometimes stagger) to their cars was an added benefit. You might just stop something before it had a chance to start.

Vonda's was a real hangout. Six nights a week the only thing louder than the crowd on the stools was the fluorescent jukebox. Her regulars knew when everywhere else was quiet and settled-in Vonda's Watering Hole was likely to be hoppin'. That Thursday evening things were true to form.

———··———

"I count three cars and two pickups in the parkin' lot...don't look like Vonda's got much going on this evenin'," said Earl Simpson, as he pulled the small handle to let his seat back a little.

"You know what, Deputy Lashe? I'd like to know just how much of our business has come out of that place over the years."

"The first arrest I made after being elected was right over there. Some character didn't like their choices in beer. So he headed in the back to check the inventory himself."

"I'll never forget slippin' and sliddin' with that drunk on the slick cooler floor, both of us goin' for a headlock at the same time."

"It wasn't Vonda's Watering Hole back then was it Sheriff?"

"No, no, it was owned by a fella named Mixon, Art Mixon, I believe. He called the place, The Beer Keg."

"But I tell ya. That old boy ran a right good business. He wouldn't put up with any shenanigans, and his patrons knew it. Since Vonda and her weasel of a husband bought him out, the place has gone to hell in a hand basket."

———..———

The Sheriff wasn't telling me a lot I didn't already know. I just liked hearing him tell a story in his easy, southern way.

He'd just asked me if I was ready to go get something to eat when Booker Griggs and his cousin came out of Vonda's place.

I didn't know either of them, but the Sheriff went way back with the Griggs clan.

Booker had messed around with everything from stolen goods to illegal liquor.

Griggs saw the Sheriff about the same time the Sheriff saw Griggs. I remember Earl sat up in the seat and Booker came to a sudden stop at his car door. Booker's cousin, whose name I don't remember, walked on around the white '62 Chevy coupe and got in on the passenger side.

I can recall sitting there for a moment or two, alternating glances between Griggs over in Vonda's parking lot and the Sheriff on my left, sitting up in an alert posture. Something was about to break loose; I just didn't know exactly what.

Then, Booker did something I can still see and hear as if it happened this morning. He continued to look at us, leaned back slightly, raised and swung a can of beer in our direction, and slowly hooted, "Yoooo Hoooo."

I knew right then there was almost certainly going to be some high-speed action; and I could've come up with a long list of officers I'd rather have seen behind the wheel than Earl. A world-class road racer he wasn't!

You see, if adjustments are to be made smoothly and under-control at high speed, a driver needs to do two very important things: sit close to the steering wheel and bend his or her arms. The Sheriff's belly didn't permit either.

I've got to admit, taunting us with the can of beer didn't do much for my attitude either. But it obviously struck a more reactionary note with Sheriff Earl. He said a couple of things that reflected badly on Booker's mother.

If those two characters had just enjoyed the moment and pulled out of Vonda's place in a slow, reasonable manner, the Sheriff may

[133]

have been able to restrain himself. But the jackrabbit exit from the parking lot pushed things over the edge.

———··———

"Eli, I think we'd be serving the residents of Tuhont County well if we had a talk with those two ol' boys," said Earl Simpson as he reached for the switch to start the Plymouth.

"Yeah, me too," replied Lashe, whispering more to himself than responding directly to his boss.

In short order, it was clear Griggs was going to run. He'd gotten well down State Highway 112 before Simpson was able to get the Plymouth backed up, turned around and headed in the right direction.

Lashe got on the radio while the cruiser was coming up to speed; "1661 to Tuhont County."

Avery Cooley was at the radio. Hearing the roar of the engine and the tone in Lashe's voice, he knew immediately a pursuit was underway.

"Go ahead '61."

"Tuhont, we're in pursuit of a white, '62 Chevrolet two-door, and we're heading south on 112 a mile below Vonda's Watering Hole."

"10-4, '61, I'll advise the state. 1665 is 10-7 at Buster's Grill. I'll get him headed in your direction."

The radio operator at the Asheford state patrol station was monitoring the county low-band.

[134]

"Tuhont, we have a unit down in the northern end of McGowan County. I'll advise 7-04 and ask he contact you directly."

"10-4, Asheford," replied Lashe, holding the mic in his left hand, while holding firmly to the armrest handle with his right.

The pieces of a multi-unit response were coming together. But the real question was how far and how fast Booker Griggs was going to run. The next few minutes would answer both questions. Given what might lay ahead, with Sheriff Earl at the wheel, Eli Lashe was hoping Booker's decision favored shorter and slower.

———··———

Comment: I wish everyone could listen in person as Eli recounts what follows. His expressions, inflections and various levels of emphasis really add to the story.

I don't remember what speeds we reached. Likely, it wasn't terribly fast. But what compounded the sense of speed were the herky-jerky movements that started in the Sheriff's shoulders, ran through his rigid arms, into the wheel and on down into the sensitive junctions of the steering assembly.

[135]

We were zigzagging our way around curves, stopping just to the left of the pavement's edge and just to the right of the centerline. Fortunately, we only met one other vehicle. I remember it clearly. That guy in the red pickup saw us coming and headed out across a field of soybeans. It looked as though he wasn't sure just how much road we'd be needing, but whatever it was he meant for us to have it.

My best hope was that we could get another unit in place to head off Griggs' BelAir. Little did I know that the unit to do the heading off would be ours!

Well before 1665 or 7-04 could get into position, Griggs turned right onto Radford Road. That's when a whole new concern began - dust.

Radford would have proven difficult to negotiate in the middle of the afternoon on a sunny day, but at speed, nearing sundown, chattering across the dirt and sparse gravel in dust thicker than yesterday's soup beans? No way!

The further we went, the thicker the dust, and the harder it was to see Booker Griggs' brake lights. Reason dictated we slow down and write off the chase to July's dry, dusty weather. But, no, not with Sheriff Earl C. Simpson having been saluted with a half-empty can of beer by one of Vonda's regulars.

I was mindful of who was driving, the boss, and I remember resisting the urge to just say something simple, something like: Sheriff, slow this thing down...NOW!

I'm glad I didn't blurt out anything, because just about that time Sheriff Earl unleashed the unexpected. In the blink of an eye, we were at a 45-degree angle to the right, jumping the ditch, and blasting through a barbed wire fence onto Robert Markey's Dairy Farm.

To the best of my memory, the Sheriff spoke his first words as we seesawed back to earth and took off again. It was one of his favorite expressions, followed by a brief apology, "Hot Dang! Sorry Eli!"

I remember opting not to answer a radio call from the county office. I was too taken by the accelerating ride across the rolling hills in the Markey pasture, the unlit cigar Earl bit in two when we came through fence, and the large, black and white Holstein cows scattering in several directions. I just knew we were going to take out one or two of Robert Markey's prized animals. Somehow we managed not to.

Perhaps the better part of a mile from where we came through the fence, we exited in similar fashion, bouncing to a stop in the middle of Radford Road. I can still recall the scratchy, clatter of barbed wire around the grill, across the hood and down the sides of the car.

Booker Griggs rounded the sweeping curve, saw our Plymouth in the middle of the road, got on the brakes hard, and went in two circles before bouncing to a stop in the left-hand ditch.

I've never really made up my mind as to whether Earl Simpson decided to head-'em-off before or after we went through that barbed wire. I really think it might have been a case of let's-just-keep-on-goin' rather than something planned beforehand. Of course, Earl spoke often of his strategic decision to set up his own roadblock.

When the Sheriff and I got to the BelAir, Booker Griggs was in the condition we'd expected - smelling like a low-rent brewery and oblivious to the trouble he was in, as evidenced by his toothy grin. Booker had never been the sharpest tool in the box.

Those of you old enough to remember early-eighties, prime time television will understand why I refer to that ride as my Dukes of Hazzard moment in law enforcement.

Millie has said more than once she wished I'd never told her this story. She's also a Yoo Hoo© fan. But now, like me, she has trouble enjoying a Yoo Hoo© without thinking about Booker Griggs and his "Yoooo Hoooo" moment.

Now that you have the picture of Booker and his chocolate-flavored salute in mind, resolve to not let it spoil your next break with a cold Yoo Hoo© and a pack of cheese crackers.

DISPOSITION

For years after the Griggs episode, Vonda's Watering Hole continued to attract some of Tuhont County's most colorful characters. It burned down in the '80's. Vonda's husband was charged with torching it for the insurance.

Several years after the dusty chase on Radford Road, Booker Griggs was badly injured in a collision with a fuel oil truck. Pertinent to the story, the accident happened when he ran one of the stop signs at the Cooper Road/SH 112 intersection - drinking of course.

I don't think I ever saw Earl Simpson madder than he was that night.

Several months after it happened I asked him why. It wasn't the Yoooo Hoooo taunting or the exhausting "bath" in adrenalin flying down a dusty, dirt road. It was something far less complicated. Getting out of the cruiser, he snagged himself on the barbed wire and torn a large triangle out of his favorite uniform pants.

Of course the county repaired Robert Markey's fences. It was a bargain compared to what Tuhont would have faced had we hit several of those purebred Holsteins.

I should also point out that one of the dairy's large black and white ladies expressed herself with a special delivery package. It took an effort to clean out the grill on that Plymouth Fury.

NOT YOUR TYPICAL TUESDAY
September 6, 1966

One evening at a dinner party, a
neighbor asked what night of the week I
remembered as being the quietest, the least
memorable from a law enforcement standpoint.
My answer was Tuesday.

Tuesday night is half way between last
Saturday's spike in activity and the spike to
come next Saturday. It's not scientific, but I'll
bet statistics will bear it out.

Be that as it may, there was one Tuesday
I'll never, ever forget. It started and ended
with two incredibly bizarre experiences. I'll
let you readers decide which one takes first
prize.

I'd never been to Feldman State Hospital
before that Tuesday morning. I went three
more times during my years with the sheriff's
department - three to drop someone off and

once to pick someone up, each time by court order.

In September of '66, Deputy Renea Raney and I were tasked with transporting Pamela Ellen Powers to Feldman pursuant to her involuntary commitment. In my first few years working with the department I'd had no dealings with the Powers family, but that changed during the trip to Jacksboro and a series of developments which followed.

According to notes provided by her doctors, Pamela was schizophrenic, manifesting itself primarily in repetitive delusions. (I don't recall the exact medical language).

I'd only scanned the summary notes before arriving at Tuhont County Hospital to pick her up. That brief reading was enough to give me pause, wondering just what Renea and

I might encounter with the troubled young woman.

When we got to the hospital, the medical staff told us she had been sedated and there should be no problem on the trip to Feldman. There were no arm or leg restraints, but I don't remember giving it a second thought. Her chin was on her chest and her hands in her lap when the nurses rolled the wooden wheelchair to the car.

When we got underway, Pamela was lying down in the back seat. She looked to be asleep. Raney and I commented on how unfortunate it was to see an attractive young woman with such severe mental problems. She married at a young age and had two small children.

The last time I told this story someone asked why she was transported in one of our cars and not in an ambulance. My answer was simple - I don't know. Typically, an ambulance was used, but that wasn't the case with Pamela Powers. I was later told her family didn't want to pay the ambulance fee. All I knew at the time was that Sheriff Simpson had called me in his office and said he wanted Renea Raney and me to get it done.

A single, 25-year-old male deputy alone with a 30-year-old, delusional female on a two-hour ride through the countryside was worse than a bad idea. Raney was assigned to go along for the obvious reasons.

Things went well for the first hour. We'd made one bathroom stop and Powers declined the opportunity. The only movement she'd made was to sit up briefly just after we got on the road, run her hands through her hair, look around, and lay back down.

The action started at our second stop, just inside the Lowesburg city limits. I pulled into a Gulf service station, turned off the engine and headed for the men's room. Having drunk the lion's share of a large Thermos of coffee, (Renea wasn't a coffee drinker) it was a matter of some urgency.

———··———

Eli tapped the hood as he rounded the front of the car walking toward the building. Deputy Raney, who was leaning over re-tying her shoe laces, looked up and nodded her understanding through the windshield.

When Renea got out and opened the right rear door, Powers was still lying in the back seat with her head on the hospital pillow and light blue blanket pulled up around her neck.

"Okay, Pamela, let's go to the bathroom, and then we'll get you that candy bar you asked for," said Raney, leaning into the open car door.

Renea later told Eli about the strange expression on Powers' face as she raised her head and looked in her direction. "It wasn't like she was looking at me; she was looking at someone behind me, more right through me. Maybe there is where I should have known something was up."

Powers jerked the blanket into the rear floorboard, and kicked the female deputy in the upper chest, knocking her to the ground. That's when Pamela jumped from the car and started to pirouette across the parking lot, buck naked.

[147]

While we had been empathizing with her condition, chatting about the passing countryside and discussing how long it might take to complete things in Jacksboro, Powers was under the blanket, quietly stripping from head to toe.

Car horns began to blow and several men stepped into the parking lot from one of the station's service bay doors.

She didn't try to run when Deputy Raney came charging from one direction and I from another. She just kept on spinning and twirling. Someone had neglected to tell us that one of her dominant delusions was that of an exotic dancer, nude if you please.

The buck-naked ballerina didn't resist at first, only smiling and laughing softly as we hurried her back toward the car. But when Renea started to get her re-dressed, the screams about being kidnapped started. The louder she screamed, the larger the crowd, both from inside the station and from the several cars that stopped on either side of the cruiser.

Our struggles, mostly outside the Dodge, had gone on for a while. This was no typical takedown. With me, there were more than a few starts and stops. I'd never seen that special section in the department's policy manual about subduing, without assaulting, a naked female.

When it came to re-dressing versus remaining in the raw, Pamela won.

Finally, Deputy Raney and I were able to get her down in the back seat, handcuffed and partially-wrapped in the blanket. For the next 40-miles, Powers rode with her legs pinned down across Raney's lap, sobbing continually, talking about her children and what were clearly haunting fears swimming in her head. Following some of the longest miles you might imagine we pulled up in front of the Feldman Hospital building.

Even with the help of hospital orderlies, getting Pamela from the car to a room and secured in a bed was only slightly less trying than the scene in front of the Gulf station. She continually cried out for someone to stop the attack, so she could finish her dance.

When Renea and I closed the car doors, we just sat there, staring straight ahead. It's no overstatement to say we were both speechless, dumbfounded by the ordeal.

To better get a feel for what we experienced, it's helpful to picture the surroundings. In those days the Feldman State Mental Hospital was housed in several weathered, dark-gray, rock buildings more than 100 years old. When considered against a backdrop like that medieval-looking place, what we'd gone through really seemed surreal.

Then came the morning's finale - a man standing on the inside ledge, of a tall, open, third-story window, holding the bars and auctioneering like crazy - no one walking on the grounds, no other cars in sight, just the oppressive look of dark, stone buildings and a patient (I trust he wasn't a member of the staff) auctioning at the top of his lungs, selling pieces of some estate that existed only in his mind.

It was 3:00 o'clock when we finally got back to Asheford. On the ride home, the numbing effects of the morning's events had begun to be replaced by the return of a gnawing sympathy for Pamela Powers. As we pulled in beside the new courthouse, Renea pointed out, for the third time, the insignificance of our morning's difficulties when compared to what lay ahead for the young mother we'd left in a distressing ward at Feldman. About that, she was most certainly correct.

> Comment: Eli's wife told me about his attempts to keep up with Pamela Powers' fate. He or Renea Raney made calls to one doctor in particular. Millie said reports varied from month to month. In his young career, the trip to Jacksboro was likely Eli's first experience with the terror of severe mental disorder in someone so young and otherwise healthy. In such cases the sickness seems even more invasive and unnatural.

Understanding the unique nature of what had taken place, Deputy Raney and I briefed the Sheriff immediately after getting back. We'd hardly begun before he called in one of the county attorneys, Mack Singleton, to listen in and take notes from a liability standpoint.

The de-briefing lasted more than an hour, and the atmosphere in the room was somber from beginning to end. Singleton's line of questioning focused on the specifics of how Pam Powers' clothes were removed, as well as how she was restrained and ultimately subdued - in great detail it seemed to me. The conversation dealt with the possibility of legal action by the family and its implications for the officers, particularly the only man involved.

Mack Singleton insisted Raney and I write our reports in separate rooms. We did, and for that I would end up being very thankful.

The schedule called for me to begin patrolling the following morning at 6:00 o'clock. I was cleared to take the cruiser home following the completion of my report.

As I prepared to turn right out of the parking lot, another county unit turned in and the deputy blinked his lights, indicating he wanted me to stop. I did, and that's when the second highly unlikely part of Tuesday, September 6, 1966 began.

———— ··· ————

Deputy Joe Collins stopped his Plymouth beside Lashe's Dodge, and rolled down his window. Eli's window was already down and the deputy's arm hanging outside the door.

Collins, the newest member of Earl Simpson's department, spun the knob, turning on the interior light. Eli saw two things at once – the man in the right corner of the back seat and the left shoulder board on Collins' uniform, hanging off the deputy's shoulder. There'd been a run-in.

"Eli, how 'bout comin' back in and givin' me a hand with this guy," said Collins, dabbing a handkerchief against a scrape on his left cheek.

Even in the yellowed glow of the Plymouth's interior light, Lashe could tell that Collins had been in a significant scuffle, presumably with the muscular-looking man in the back.

Eli didn't respond, he just put the Dodge in reverse and backed around into the parking spot he'd just left. Collins drove straight to the side entrance of the new courthouse, which led to the booking area. Not until Eli got over to Collins' cruiser could he tell just how scuffed up the young deputy really was. His badge was in his right hand; most of his shirt tail was out and stained with blood; a shirt pocket was torn lose and hanging in front of his chest, and there were two, large torn places in his uniform pants, one framing a badly skinned knee.

The two officers went around to the passenger side rear door and took Hoyt Wheeler out of the car. He stood well over six feet, was shaved completely bald, with broad shoulders and an unusually small, athletic-looking waist. There was a shoe and sock on his left foot and nothing on his right. He was bleeding from both elbows, as well as around one wrist where the cuff had bitten deeply into the skin.

If two men hadn't jumped into the fray to help subdue the subject, Joe Collins might have faced a far more serious outcome in his efforts to put Wheeler under arrest.

As both officers held an arm walking toward the jail, Lashe saw that Wheeler was handcuffed in front rather than behind his back. Joe had probably done the best he could do under the circumstances, and Eli wasn't about to suggest removing the cuffs and replacing them behind the subject – not judging from what appeared to have gone on earlier.

——— ·•· ———

As Joe and I walked Wheeler between the two glass doors, Chauncey Cobb was waiting at the circular counter, where he was most of the time, day or night. He had no family other

[155]

than a brother, who lived somewhere out west.
Even during his time off the life-long Tuhont
County resident was most often at or near the
new courthouse. He'd been the chief jailer for
years and was conscientious in his duties.

I hope you readers will permit me to
sidestep here. I want to let you know a little
more about Chauncey.

He was as likable a guy as you'll ever
meet. The only other interest he had was
fishing, and he loved it. He'd invited me along
two or three times since I'd jointed the
department. To watch Chauncey Cobb work a
live spring lizard on the end of a long,
active, fly rod, was poetry in motion.

I gladly paddled and watched from the
back bench while Chauncey stood and fished
from the bow, finding the sweet spot along a
shallow point or between two submerged
stumps; then bending over slightly and

feeding out the bright orange line as the bass took the lizard toward deeper water.

It was intriguing to watch Chauncey manage the rod and line, hook, fight, and land a nice bass - with one hand. At birth, his left arm extended only 5 or 6 inches below the elbow.

A machinist friend fabricated a padded half-circle rest for his left forearm and attached it to the bottom of his fly rod, 20-inches above the butt's cork padding. His right hand engaged or disengaged a spring-loaded reel, which aided the casting and retrieval actions. It was quite a rig and he was quite a fisherman.

The motivation for the extra steps he'd taken to master the technique had come from deep within Chauncey's childhood. He'd grown up with an older cousin constantly telling him he'd never be able to fish with that

[157]

"stump of an arm". He only told me about the cousin's goading predictions once, but it stuck, along with his summary comment - "I reckon he was wrong."

Now, I'll get back to the story.

None of us had run across Hoyt Wheeler before that memorable Tuesday in '66 and together we knew just about all the area's tough guys. He was a new one.

The run-in had occurred when Joe answered a call to a small, but well-known honky-tonk in the extreme southeast corner of the county. I'd only been there once, on a disturbance call. It had pretty much flamed out by the time I arrived. But there's no question, the place was known for rough stuff from time to time.

When Joe pulled up, the owner was holding sway with a shotgun. Before the double-barrel came out from under the bar, Wheeler had been slapping two guys around.

The struggle between Collins and Wheeler started when Joe tried to put cuffs on the big guy.

No one, with the possible exception of Hoyt Wheeler, knew the second fracas was only moments away.

———··———

The two deputies put their weapons in the lockbox and walked on either side of Wheeler heading down the right cellblock hallway. Cobb, as he often did, was walking just behind, jingling two large, brass key rings.

They stopped at cell #6, where Chauncey stepped around, inserted and turned the heavy, metal key. Cobb pulled open the door and stepped to the right.

That's when Hoyt Wheeler reached above his head and grabbed the heavy bar that served as the cross member of the steel door frame. Lashe and Collins reacted immediately, pulling and hacking downward at the prisoner's elbows. The harder they tried, the more he twisted both arms inward, stepped back and spread his feet, increasing his rigid and braced position. The cuffs held his hands, wrists and forearms close together,

[159]

making it even more difficult to break Wheeler's hold on the overhead bar.

Initially, Lashe was working from the right and Collins from the left. Following what was little progress, Collins got his right arm around Wheeler's neck, pulling back and down.

"Turn loose, Hoyt! Turn loose of the bars!" shouted Joe Collins, while Lashe drove his shoulder into the prisoner's right side. Wheeler was a powerful, determined man. He was angry, strangely silent, slick with sweat, and determined to take on the officers' best effort.

If possible, Lashe and Collins wanted to avoid hitting Wheeler with fists or Billy Clubs. That reservation wasn't shared by Chauncey Cobb.

Cobb pulled the Billy Club from Lashe's belt and went to work on Wheeler's biceps and forearms. Three or four strong, bruising licks and he turned loose. The hold-on-to-the-bars contest quickly turned into a balancing act just outside the cell door, Lashe and Collins pinning Wheeler's arms against his chest and trying to force him into the cell, one small, sideways, step at a time.

Chauncey dropped the baton and began using his left shoulder and right hand to help the deputies push the man's upper torso. In an instant, his hand slipped up and over Wheeler's sweaty shoulder, straight into the prisoner's mouth.

———···———

I thought a .22 had gone off.

Before Chauncey could get his hand out of that guy's mouth, he'd bitten off the first two digits of the ring finger of Cobb's right hand. I don't believe it would've been any cleaner if a hatchet had been used.

Ol' Chauncey yelled and backed away from the cell door, bouncing up against the cement block wall. Collins and I stopped; so did Wheeler. We watched as Chauncey dug the handkerchief out of his right rear pocket, while trying to avoid using what was left of the finger.

Chauncey moaned several times before looking up with pure rage in his eyes. In a flash, he charged, taking all three of us into the cell and onto the bunk. Still trying to protect the injured finger, he got the slapjack out of Collins' pocket, turned it edgeways and drew blood with every lick. He chopped with the slapjack on the right side

[161]

of Wheeler's head and shoulder while driving the end of his left arm into his neck and chest.

I recall lying on the cot on my right side with my arms still locked around Wheeler, not knowing whether I should hold on or turn loose and try to get Chauncey under control. It took both Joe and I to stop the slapjack and blood from flying.

We got Cobb out to the car where it was decided I would stay at the jail and Collins would drive him to the hospital. As we put him in on the passenger's side, Chauncey muttered, "Somebody go get my finger." That old boy had more presence of mind than Joe and I put together.

When I got back to the cell, Hoyt Wheeler was sitting up on the bunk, a bloody mess. He just sat there, grinning while I looked around for Cobb's missing finger.

[162]

Then he said, "Hey, you."

I looked up. He reached down beside his right leg, picked up what I was looking for, and pitched it through the bars. I'll never forget how bizarre he looked, smiling and tossing me the front half of Chauncey Cobb's already chalky-looking finger.

When I finally got to the hospital, Cobb was in surgery. Joe Collins told me he couldn't get over how many shots they'd given our jailer. The doctors said the possibility of bacterial infection from a human bite was much higher than people might expect.

Now, if you've ever had a wilder Tuesday than I did on September 6, 1966 - don't believe I want to hear about it.

DISPOSITION

We heard much more from Pamela Powers' family about her abuse and mistreatment on the trip to Jacksboro than we did about hoped-for improvement in her health. They hired counsel and a couple of dispositions were taken. There was money for an attorney, but not for a comfortable ambulance ride to the hospital. Imagine that.

Our separately-prepared reports, compatible written statements and corroborating witness testimony didn't favor the family getting any sort of financial settlement from the county. The suit never got off the ground.

Pamela was finally transferred to an extended-care facility. I never heard any more after that.

It turned out <u>Hoyt Wheeler</u> was a bad guy just passing through on his way to Louisiana. He had violations in both Virginias, a couple of other states, as well as Puerto Rico, where he grew up. He was charged with felony maiming, among other things, convicted, and sent off for more than a few years for the assault on Collins and Cobb.

Less than a year later, Joe Collins left the department and moved out of state. It turned out that things had gotten pretty rough before the two guys helped subdue Wheeler. A medical exam determined something in his throat had been damaged, and bad headaches followed. It's my guess his young, pregnant wife had a lot to do with Joe's resignation.

Chauncey Cobb ended up losing most of the finger. He seemed to take it harder than you might have thought. But in the end, it didn't slow him down. He got back to fishing - thankfully with me along on a few occasions.

ONE NIGHT ON INDIANA AVENUE

January 15, 1967

It might have been more to the point if the title of this story had been "Another Night on Indiana Avenue", or "One of Many Nights on Indiana Avenue", or "Please, Not Again on Indiana Avenue". There were far more than one, when our cars spent time in a driveway on that road.

From cursing out the windows to rolling in the street, it seemed like something or someone was always stirred up.

Of the 8 to 10 houses there, two in particular were most often in play - the Stiners and the Sewells. Merlin Stiner and Rico Sewell were first cousins and bitter enemies. The only fortunate thing about their relationship was that Merlin lived on one end and Rico on the other. Often, that wasn't enough to keep them apart.

[167]

On a cold January night in '67, it was Rico Sewell that proved the problem. I'd dealt more with Merlin Stiner than I had with the Sewell family. But I knew Rico could be every bit as ornery as his older cousin.

Tate Taft and I were putting fuel in the cruiser at the county maintenance shed when the call came in.

———··———

"Tuhont County to 1665."

Taft put the oil measurement stick back in its tube, opened the driver's door and snapped the mic loose from its mount.

"Go ahead, County."

"'65 what's your 20?"

"We're gassing up at the maintenance shed."

"10-4, we've got a call from 204 Indiana Avenue. A subject, Martha Sewell, reports her husband is drunk and shooting a gun in the house. She says they need officers there at once. That's 204 Indiana Avenue, subject calling is Martha Sewell."

Tate shook his head before answering. "10-4, we're on our way." Taft put the mic back on the clip like he meant for it to stay, before shouting for Eli Lashe to hurry up. Lashe was in one of the outhouses near the rolling equipment parking lot.

Eli jogged toward the back of the car, wondering what was up. "What we got Tate?"

"We got a call over on Indiana Avenue."

Lashe's reply was subdued, but to the point.

"Damn."

Taft and Lashe headed for the notorious stretch of road with siren and emergency lights engaged. Although they responded in a manner consistent with a shots-fired call, neither officer looked forward to another round with Rico Sewell. They knew him, and the address, all too well.

————··————

When we turned onto Indiana the first thing we saw was Rico's wife, some man and another woman waiting on the corner. I remember noticing right off a small child in Martha Sewell's arms. In the middle of January, the little boy was wearing only a pair of pajamas.

Mrs. Sewell was in bedroom slippers and a housecoat. It was obvious she'd grabbed the child and left the house in a hurry. The temperature was near freezing, and both were trembling when Tate and I got to them.

My first impulse was to look for Rico Sewell, make sure he wasn't in the bushes or behind a tree. The last time some of our folks arrested the scoundrel, he'd led them on a muddy footrace through the woods behind his house. I'm sure the only reason we weren't shot at that night, was the fact he didn't have a gun. In the next few minutes we were going to learn better.

———···———

Martha Sewell's eyes were red and swollen as she bounced the eighteen-month-old higher up on her shoulder.

"He's been drinking all day and this time he nearly killed me and Ricky. You gotta do somethin' 'bout him! Get him out of the house! Please go in there and arrest him!" cried Martha Sewell. She was standing only inches from both officers.

"Mrs. Sewell, calm down please, tell us what he did and when he did it," said Eli Lashe.

"I asked him to please stop drinkin' and shoutin' so much. He was frightenin' our son. So, he slapped me on the side of my head and said he was gonna kill me. He went to the closet, got his gun, and started shootin' all over the place. He was yellin' and kickin' over furniture. Please, please, go get him!"

"And when did he do this, Mrs. Sewell?" asked Lashe.

That's when the man spoke up for the first time. He'd been edging closer as Martha Sewell described her husband's actions. It was clear he wanted to get in on the conversation.

"It happened about an hour ago, deputy! What difference does that make?"

Tate Taft turned, his look as edgy as the man's question – "and, you're who, sir?"

He identified himself as Martha Sewell's brother and said the other woman was his wife. Martha had called them from a neighbor's house.

Taft turned slowly back toward Rico's wife.

"Mrs. Sewell, we can't just go in your house and arrest your husband. We need a warrant to arrest someone when we don't catch them in the course of committing an illegal act."

Before Lashe and Taft arrived, Martha Sewell's brother had clearly worked himself up in front of the women, talking big and threatening to take on the task of dealing with Rico all by himself.

"What the hell is this? You can't go in and arrest him for what he's done? Maybe I need to go in there and take care of that drunk myself! I'm sick and tired of how

[171]

he treats her. He's not the only one that owns a gun. Hell fire, I can do it with my bare hands."

Both Lashe and Taft were incensed by the haughty claim. Each knew Rico Sewell and each could see Rico going up one side of his brother-in-law and down the other like a buzz saw.

Taft was known for having a short fuse and the words struck a match. "Sir, you're not gonna use your fists or guns to take on anyone tonight. If you want to help, get your sister, wife and this little boy somewhere they can warm up. But right this moment, you're gonna close your mouth, while we explain to Mrs. Sewell what must take place if we're going to enter that house and arrest Rico. You understand?" The man nodded his agreement.

While Taft clued-in Martha Sewell's brother, Eli went to the patrol car to get a blanket from the trunk. "Here, put this around yourself and your son," said Lashe, placing it across Martha Sewell's shoulders and pulling it together in front. The little boy continued to tremble, even under the thick, green wrap.

——— ••• ———

I guess it was the trembling lower lip that drew me so hard toward the child. Tate and I were standing there listening to his outraged mother make all sorts of demands and his uncle talking tough, while the little

[172]

boy looked to be freezing to death. Before the conversation continued, Tate and I got the four of them into the backseat of the cruiser and cranked up the heater.

After knocking the chill off, we explained again why the warrant was necessary and only a judge could handle that at 30-minutes past midnight on a Sunday morning. They wanted to know what judge and how he could be reached.

And, therein lay the rub. The judge's name was Bernard Willowford and both of us knew His Honor wouldn't take kindly to getting a call in the wee hours of the morning. He was short on patience and long on temper, a testier individual behind the bench you were not likely to meet.

Martha Sewell, even two hours after the incident, was still very angry and determined to have her husband arrested. Her brother's ugly talk didn't help calm things down either.

As you would expect, Tate and I were very reluctant to give those three Judge Willowford's phone number, but they were determined and I guess we felt obligated to help.

I reluctantly radioed the office, got the number, jotted it down on a piece of paper, and handed it to Martha Sewell. All three adults were quickly out of the car and headed back down Indiana. Our offer to take them somewhere was promptly rejected.

Before resuming our patrol, the last thing I remember was that little boy in our headlights looking back from his mother's shoulder under the edge of that army blanket. We both hoped they might go back to the brother's house, warm up, and let Rico sleep it off, but no such luck.

———··———

It was going on 2:00 AM when the two deputies received the call they hoped might not come.

"Tuhont County to 1665."

"There it is," said Eli as he put the mic to his mouth.

"Go ahead, Tuhont County."

"65 Martha Sewell called and said she has the warrant you requested. She said they are waiting on the corner for you to return. She didn't say who 'they' were. Are you familiar with the situation?"

"10-4 Tuhont, we're familiar and we're en route."

Before Lashe could get the round disk on the back of the mic into its snap cradle, the second part of the Tuhont County message came in.

"And 65, here's one for you, Judge Willowford wants you to call him at home. I took him to mean as soon as you get this message. I have the number if you're ready to copy."

"Tuhont, we've got the number."

The deputies stopped at a 7-11 store, where Tate Taft made the call. The Judge answered within two seconds of the first ring. His words were immediate and angry.

"Is this Taft or Lashe?"

"This is Deputy Taft, Your Honor."

"...two things for you Taft: here's number one...don't you ever, ever have someone call me in the

[175]

middle of the night again! You understand number one, don't you?"

"Yes sir, I fully understand."

"...and here's number two: you ever give my home phone number out again, and I'll rain so much crap down on you, you'll need a hat! You understand number two, as well, right?"

"Yes sir, I fully understand."

"And, you make sure your partner, Eli Lashe, gets the same two-part message!"

"Yes sir, will do."

——— ··· ———

I don't remember if Tate and I exchanged a single word heading back to meet Martha Sewell, probably not, we weren't really that far away. Plus, the whole scene had turned into something best served by restraint, verbal and otherwise.

As promised, all three were on the same corner, Martha's brother with his foot back up on the fire hydrant and his hands sitting on his hips. The little boy had been left with a neighbor.

I recall Martha's brother being a short, heavy-set guy, with a scruffy beard and over-done gold necklace. In my opinion, the long, thin cigar in his mouth at 2:00 o'clock in the morning didn't really help with the look he was after.

As we stood there while Tate looked over the warrant, the guy brought up again going in the house himself. It was that second display of swagger that really hit me wrong. I told him we'd be happy to have him go with us; in fact he could lead the way if he felt that would help.

Rather quickly he changed his tune, and we all agreed someone needed to stay behind to look after the ladies.

The paperwork was in order. I remember thinking Judge Willowford's hit-and-miss attempt at a signature probably reflected his irritation at the time he signed the warrant.

We asked Martha Sewell several questions, confirming three things: the layout of the house, the fact that Rico had three guns, a pistol and two long guns, and the fact that he'd been drinking most all day and was, to use her words, "mean drunk".

When we got back in the car to ride down Indiana toward the third house on the right, Tate and I knew the situation would be high-risk. Rico Sewell had proven capable of hurting someone even when he was stone-cold sober, much less when he was, "mean drunk".

———··———

The small, white house was rectangular, with two windows on the front, one on each side of the door and a five-foot-square cement landing under a single, low-watt bulb. The backside was the same. There were no windows on either end of the house.

The two deputies eased into the driveway and Lashe turned off the engine.

No lights were on except the two outside bulbs, favoring anyone wanting to look out and no one wanting to look in. There would be no sneaking up on Rico

Sewell. What made the situation even more unnerving was what appeared to be two bullet holes in the bottom pane of one front window.

"What ya think, Eli?"

"...don't know just what to think. I know I don't like it a bit. We're sittin' ducks if he wants to shoot first and talk later."

"Yeah, I know it. Well, let's slip around here to the right and take a look out back," suggested Taft. Both men got out, eased the doors closed, drew their weapons and started to move toward the back yard along a head-high row of bushes to the right of the driveway. They stopped just inside the shadow created where the rear corner blocked off the back porch light.

After pulling his head and shoulders back into the shadow, Taft summed things up: "Hell, same as around front, plenty of light outside and none inside. Looks to me like we're just gonna have to get on that porch and go in like family."

Comment: Although Eli didn't include it he's told me before about the scare they got. He said it's a wonder they hadn't shot up the whole place when a cat came off the top of Sewell's '56 Ford Fairlane, jumped onto the hood and tore off into the bushes.

————··————

There was no strategy behind choosing the back door over the front; it may have been just that the rear door was closer. They both represented very poor options.

I'll tell you one thing for sure; I don't believe I've ever felt more like the end might come any second than I did going up on that small cement pad, turning the knob and easing that door open. Not quite as bad as me, but Tate was wet with perspiration, even on a cold January night. If he wanted to start some real trouble, everything favored Sewell.

Ol' Tate was right behind me, as close as he could get trying to go in at the same time I did. Of course the door was not wide enough for both of us to be first in line. There was never a doubt he would back me up, as I would him. But that didn't do much to take the charge out of the air.

We stepped into a small kitchen, where light coming through the open door stopped at the archway leading into the living room. To our right, there was a shotgun lying on the yellow Formica-top of a metal dinette table.

Beyond the table a doorway led down a hall toward two bedrooms and a single bath.

We'd agreed to use only our flashlights once in the house, hoping to shine them in Sewell's eyes if he popped out from around a corner or door. We hadn't discussed it, but there was every likelihood either one of us could've shot Rico Sewell on the spot, if it came to that.

When I think about going into that house, there's always something that comes to mind. It's funny how certain things stick in your head. Once inside I was struck by the strangest of smells. If you can imagine, it was the combined smell of used beer and gun powder. Neither seemed stronger than the other, but both registered when I took a breath.

The dried heave was on the table and several places on the floor. Bullet holes were all over the ceiling, as well as in the walls and refrigerator door. The kitchen curtains were in the sink and all four kitchen chairs were overturned - one with two of the legs driven through the drywall just above the base shoe molding.

Even on Sunday night, Indiana Avenue may have been the only street in Tuhont County where that much residential ruckus and shooting could go on and not a single neighbor would take time to call the law.

———··———

Tate Taft kept his voice low. "Eli, let's stay together. I'll focus left of center and you to the right. Let's look in the living room first."

They turned on their flashlights – as agreed, Tate's beam moved to the left and Eli's to the right. There were more bullet holes and a turned over coffee table, but no Rico Sewell. Next, there were the bedrooms.

"Sheriff's department, we have a warrant, Mr. Sewell," announced Eli Lashe as the two deputies moved slowly down the twenty-foot hall. "Sheriff's department, Rico," echoed Taft moving quickly to look in the bedroom on the right.

You know you're a regular customer when all the deputies can call you by your first name.

Again, inspections which included a closet in the hall, one in each bedroom, along with the underside of two beds didn't turn up Rico Sewell.

The bathroom door was pulled open by Taft, who jumped quickly back to the right. Lashe was down low on the left of the door opening. The shower curtain was torn down, and the commode had more dried heave on it, than in it. He'd certainly been there earlier that night, but the deputies were again thwarted in their efforts to find and arrest Rico Sewell.

———··———

After we'd cleared the house, Tate and I turned on what lights still had bulbs. That's when we really got a look at what Martha Sewell meant by "mean drunk". Lighting fixtures had been knocked from the ceiling; what appeared to have been a rifle butt was used to cave in places on many of the walls; the television screen was kicked or knocked

[183]

in; and a dozen or more dishes had been slammed into the kitchen floor.

The inside of that house was a scene where it was difficult to tell the difference between "plain old crazy as a loon" and "plain old mean as hell". We gave the house a second going-over and then got back to the business at hand - finding Rico Sewell and his other two weapons.

———— ... ————

"Eli, you think he could've just taken off?"

"No...I don't think so," replied Lashe staring at the pair of shoes sitting by the couch. "I don't think he would've taken off in freezing weather without his shoes, and the car is still in the driveway."

The thought hit Tate only an instant before it hit Eli Lashe – *the car!* Maybe he was planning on taking off, and the front seat was as far as Rico Sewell could get.

Taft's pistol and flashlight reached the driver's window at the same time Lashe's light and Smith & Wesson muzzle arrived on the passenger's side.

There was Rico Sewell, behind the wheel, slumped over to the right, dead to the world. A revolver was in his right hand and a rifle was in the back seat. In the final analysis, it was beer and booze that brought things to a manageable end.

———...———

I opened the door, eased the pistol from his hand and slipped the cuffs on. His only resistance amounted to two grunts and one dry heave.

That's when the flood of relief comes, dragging a jerk like that to his feet, after being fortunate enough to avoid a bullet or load of shot. What you need to be careful of is not letting powerful relief turn into undue force. In the pre-dawn hours on that cold Sunday morning at the eastern end of Indiana Avenue, it wasn't easy.

DISPOSITION

Oh my, how quickly some mistreated wives can make an emotional turnaround after an ugly episode with their husband, especially when she sees him being cuffed and loaded into the back of a sheriff's car. Martha

<u>Sewell</u>, her brother and sister-in-law were waiting in the front yard when Tate and I came around the house. With our hands driven up under Rico's arms, his shoulders were level with his forehead and his toes barely touching the ground.

Rico's wife was crying when she asked if we had to take him away. She carried on about how some of it may have been her fault. She expressed worries about their son without his daddy around, and on and on it went. Once we got Rico in the back seat, Tate turned to Martha Sewell and spoke for both of us; "Lady, this un's goin' to jail!"

However, the Sewells may have had the last laugh. He received little more than a shame-on-you from <u>Judge Willowford</u>. The Judge insisted Tate and I both attend the hearing. No doubt he was thinking about that late-night call when he showed Rico Sewell the door. He never got another vote from me - not that he had before.

One final thing on Rico Sewell - a few years after Tate and I took him off Indiana Avenue he was pulled from his house for the last time. Some very serious people he owed a significant amount of money didn't bother with a judge.

OUR 4th WEDDING ANNIVERSARY
May 11, 1967

The following story is not very long. But for me the experience easily meets the criteria of out-of-the-ordinary.

Millie and I had dinner reservations for 7:30 at the Starlite Steak House. It was our 4th wedding anniversary, and, as luck would have it, I drew the long shift in the southern end of the county. I left the house at 5:00 AM that morning and didn't get back to the office until almost 4:30 that afternoon.

The paper trail on two domestic disturbance calls and a trespassing dust-up put me past 5:00 PM heading for the door and the 20-minute ride home.

I don't remember where everyone was when the phone rang for the 4th time. Avery Cooley must have been somewhere in the back. So, I picked it up.

———··———

"Sheriff's office, Deputy Lashe."

"Yes, yes, please, this is Juanita Deaton and we need some help right away, quickly please, out here on Larkin Road."

Mrs. Deaton, the elderly widow of past county commission chairman, Sam Deaton, was very distressed; her voice was breaking and her words were rushed. Lashe had met her several times, as had most of Sheriff' Simpson's personnel.

"Mrs. Deaton, this is Eli Lashe."

"Oh, yes, Eli, I'm on my porch and a dog is attacking my next door neighbor. Oh, my goodness, she's trying to keep it away with a stick, but it has her backed up against the chicken pen. It looks like her leg is bleeding. Please, come help her!"

A quick glance at the radio log confirmed that the only car close was tied up on another call. Given the frantic nature of Juanita Deaton's words, Lashe had only one option.

———— ··· ————

I knew Mrs. Deaton and her husband had always been great friends of the department. Sam Deaton and Earl Simpson were deputies together, before Earl ran for sheriff and Sam later was elected to the county commission. Our long relationship with the Deaton household was certainly part of what led me to drop what I was doing and take off for Larkin Road.

As you can imagine, hustling west on CR 2310 my thoughts were bouncing between an anniversary dinner with Millie and Mrs. Deaton's pleas. But assigning priority wasn't difficult. I knew Mrs. Deaton and her neighbors were about the same age and the thought of a dog going after a lady that advanced in years was very concerning.

Another issue I faced turning onto Larkin was exactly where I was headed. There were houses on both sides of the Deaton home and each was owned by an older couple.

Juanita answered that question for me.

Slowing, I saw her in her wheelchair holding the screened door open and motioning to the next house down the road - the residence of Carl and Mira Moore. Carl was a retired farmer and Mira a housekeeper. None of their children still lived at home.

I pulled into the driveway and ran to the left between the Moore and Deaton houses. As I neared the back corner the sounds I heard were a mixture of high-pitched yelps, snarls and whines. There were no barks or growls. If it was a dog, it sounded small and more frenzied than angry.

———···———

Mrs. Deaton moved back to the end of the screened-in porch to watch as Eli ran toward the Moore's back yard. She was yelling directions.

"Deputy, she's out back! She's on the ground next to the chicken coop. Hurry! Please, hurry!"

Mira Moore was on her left side, crying and trying to cover her face. The fox had her cane in its mouth, shaking its head and jumping straight up in a bowed, contorted way.

Mira Moore was bleeding from her right arm and right leg. It was clear she'd been bitten several times by the rabid animal, which ran in tight circles between its exaggerated leaps.

Lashe pulled his pistol and drew down on the fox, holding the weapon with both hands and trying to get a shot when there was plenty of daylight between Moore and the crazed canid. He never got comfortable enough to shoot.

Eli ran several steps closer to the chicken coop and shouted, "Hey, get back! Get back! Get away from her!" At first, the fox seemed unaware of the deputy, continuing to shake its head and spin in circles before dropping to its chest and flattening out from the tip of its nose to the tip of its tail.

That's when it jerked and twisted its head to the left in a sudden, strange way. The fox seemed to glare at Lashe before it charged.

———————— ··· ————————

I took my first shot as the fox ran toward me. It was my first miss.

The only thing that permitted me to get up into the bed of that hay wagon before the fox got to my legs was the fact that it was stumbling with every other step, and I was running as hard and straight as I could.

It went under the wagon and started gnawing on one of the front spokes.

Leaning over the right side of the old splintered bed, I took my second shot. It was my second miss. The bullet hit the metal band around the wooden wheel and ricocheted through the bottom of a washtub leaning against the barn.

For the first time the fox sat still, the only movement being a distraught shaking of its head. Then suddenly, it took off toward the front corner of the house, where it sat down again, bobbing its head and shoulders up and down.

It was the first and only time I've ever seen a rabid animal. It's a frightening experience. Every movement, even the slightest, seemed sudden, exaggerated, disjointed.

So, there we were. Poor Mrs. Deaton bleeding on the ground, me on my knees in the back of a hay wagon, and that fox starting and stopping, apparently trying to decide who or what to attack next.

That's when it happened - the thing I could never have foreseen. I had just jumped down from the wagon and taken my third shot, also a miss, when the explosion happened.

I nearly jumped out of my skin! I was focused on the fox as the wad of heavy shot kicked up a cloud of dust and sent the animal tumbling to its right. It took a couple of seconds for me to get my bearings and figure out what had happened.

White smoke drew my attention to Juanita Deaton's living room window. She'd gotten her husband's old 28-gauge shotgun; put in a shell (likely as old as the gun itself), jabbed the muzzle through the window screen and taken things into her own hands.

Mrs. Deaton's next shout across the yard came in the form of a question, "Did I get him?"

Indeed she did.

[195]

DISPOSITION

It took a series of painful shots, along with several stitches for <u>Mira Moore</u> to get over that terrible experience. Her husband, who was returning from a trip to take a sick calf to the vet when the attack occurred, told folks his wife showed the tooth-scared cane every time she told the story.

Mrs. Deaton's actions made all the papers, and her reputation as "Dead Eye Deaton" was born.

Millie and I didn't get to the Starlite Steak House until 9:00 o'clock, but the filets were great and our 4th anniversary saved.

There's one other follow-up here. Three shots and three misses sent me to the shooting range the following weekend.

<u>BE ON THE LOOKOUT - FOR ANYTHING</u>
June 25, 1967

I remember Sheriff Simpson for many
things - his fairness, the love he always
showed for his family, his commitment to his
officers and community, his obvious emphasis
on encouragement rather than criticism, and
of course his wit and easy-going ways. He told
and loved good jokes, particularly his own. No
one enjoyed laughing at Earl Simpson's jokes
more than Earl Simpson.

There were two wall plaques in his
office I always thought had a lot to say
about the comfortable and comforting way
Earl dealt with everyone:

<u>ALWAYS LAUGH AT THE BOSS' JOKES - IT COULD BE
SOME SORT OF LOYALTY TEST</u>

<u>IF PLAN "A" FAILS, REMEMBER, YOU HAVE 25 MORE
LETTERS</u>

One of his off-the-wall antics started a
couple of years after I'd joined the force. It

[197]

was something he did every few weeks or so for about a year, until we finally figured out what he was up to.

Driving home in the evening, he'd pick out some random vehicle, make up a partial or full license plate, along with a related story, and call it in. He'd tell everyone to be on the lookout for the car, in connection with whatever misdeeds he'd come up with, and then he'd go on to the house.

All night, we'd look for a fictitious vehicle and license plate combination. I suppose it did make us pay a little more attention to detail and increase the coverage in our patrols, but some thought it put the Sheriff in the same position as the little boy who cried wolf. Should he ever want to issue a genuine lookout, no one would take it seriously. But let me say, I could never conceive of any officer not taking Sheriff

Earl Simpson seriously when it came to enforcing the law in Tuhont County.

One night he slipped up a little. He started radioing in his lookout notice without having a clear vehicle description and story in mind. It went something like - be on the lookout for, uh, uh, be on the lookout for anything! Those words became a catchphrase among the deputies - "be on the lookout...for anything!"

And they couldn't have been more relevant than they were the afternoon Tate Taft and I went to pick up Lonnie Granville.

On June 1st, 1967 Tate became Tuhont County's first officer to wear the title "Detective". The same day he was promoted, I made sergeant. In 1967, the department consisted of Sheriff Earl Simpson, Chief Deputy Dan Simpson, Detective Tate Taft, Sgt. Howard Bone, Sgt. Eli Lashe, 8 deputies, 2 crime scene technicians, 2 office clerks and 2 jailers.

It was a good group, and everyone got along well, but if I'm honest, the officer I most enjoyed working with was Tate Taft. I was very pleased by his promotion to detective. He was a top officer who knew the business.

———— ·· ————

Taft and Lashe were headed for Hughes Trailer Park north of Asheford. The mobile home development was well above average, trimmed-out and well done. The owner, Dillon Hughes, had always made an attempt to carefully screen the people to whom he rented his units. Compared to similar properties, the sheriff's office had received a minimal number of calls over the years.

On the way, the officers discussed everything from the beautiful Sunday afternoon weather to the National Crime Information Center, which the FBI had introduced in January of that year. The conversation was lighthearted and cordial, covering everything but the pending meeting with Lonnie Granville.

Lonnie was in his early-thirties, Hollywood-handsome, from a good middle-class family, with above-average intelligence, and a knack for being a real creep.

Since his early twenties he'd been in a variety of bad situations, including stolen goods, statutory rape, bad checks, simple assault and drugs. There was some evidence he'd even been involved in child pornography – something new in the mid-sixties around Tuhont County.

In each scrape, Tate Taft had tried to be of help. But it was getting more and more difficult. Tuhont County's new Detective had run out of patience with his former high school teammate, the quarterback to whom he'd snapped the ball for three years.

As the officers neared the park, Taft was finishing a summary briefing on his experiences with Lonnie Granville. "I don't know Eli, he's always been the sort of guy that just couldn't stay out of trouble – if it wasn't one shortcut to easy money it was another; if it wasn't this shenanigan over here it was that scam over there."

"His latest stunt really got to me. Up in Polumbo County he charmed a 17-year-old into marrying him. I'll guarantee you he greased back that thick, black ducktail, unbuttoned the two top buttons on his silky shirt, promised her anything, hauled her off to some quickie chapel and married the girl. From what I've heard her family nearly went through the roof," added Taft as he and Eli pulled up in front of mobile home lot B12.

Taft felt a Sunday afternoon was the best time to find him at home.

———···———

Let me assure you, when Lonnie answered the door, he didn't look much like the "operator" Tate had described. He was beer drunk, barefooted, wearing worn-out jeans and a stained t-shirt. There was a bottle of some cheap brew in his hand. His ducktail was going in several directions, apparently a little low on it customary overdose of Brylcreem.

He acted glad to see us, but his words were inflated and his handshake overdone. I noticed Taft responding to the attempt at a hug with only a quick pat on Granville's right side.

It really wasn't a time for niceties; we were there to talk about something he and Tate had discussed several times before - a warrant. But that day things were going to end differently; that Sunday afternoon he was going to come with us. The days of allowing him to come in on his own were over. There was nothing further Tate could do to dissuade prosecutors and plaintiffs from pressing charges while he tried to help Lonnie work things out.

––––– ··· –––––

Lashe moved to the end of the couch near the side hallway leading back to the bedrooms. Taft and Granville took chairs backed up against the half partition separating the kitchen from the living room.

"Tate, you two guys want a beer, or somethin'?" asked Lonnie, looking and sounding awkward.

"No, we're on duty, and we don't need a beer. We're here to give you some bad news, Lonnie. The $200.00 check you wrote the folks at Carter's Auto Care bounced, and they've taken out a warrant for your arrest."

Eli couldn't tell whether the shocked look on Granville's face was real or faked. Most of his words and expressions carried the exaggeration typical of a con artist.

"Oh, come on man, I talked to those guys about that and told 'em I'd take care of it. They haven't taken out a damn warrant have they?"

Lashe took the paper from his shirt pocket and pitched it on the small, maple coffee table.

All three men sat silently for a moment. Granville didn't bother to look at the warrant.

"Tate, let me go by tomorrow and talk to James Carter. I know we can work this out."

"No, can't do it, Lonnie. James said he didn't want to talk to you again. That was the third bad check you've written those people, and they intend to pursue things this time. You're gonna have to come with us today. Even the judge took the time to make that point with me."

Lashe hadn't said a word since entering the door and replying to Granville's welcome with a soft, "Mornin'". The longer he watched the exchange between Detective Taft and Granville, the greater his uncertainty about what lay ahead.

Granville's words were growing louder and more emphatic. "You're gonna come in here and drag me out of my house on a Sunday afternoon on some two-bit check charge? If you would've called me, I would've cleared it up, taken them the cash or somethin'. This is bullshit, Taft! Bullshit!"

Eli watched as the two had a conversation so much like the ones they'd had in the past. This time, however, the growing tension was obvious. Having emptied the four beer bottles on the kitchen table and continuing to work on the one in his hand, Granville was sounding more-and-more like a mouthy drunk, and Tate Taft was simply loosing what little patience he had left.

Tate stood and motioned for Granville to do the same.

That's when the fourth person in the trailer stepped quickly from the hall to the end of the couch. There had been no sound from the other end of the

[204]

mobile home, no movement, no pops or cracks from the floor or walls – nothing. Suddenly, she was just there!

Almost bouncing to the edge of his chair, Granville shouted, "Kill him, Kill him!" A frightened, unsure, seventeen-year-old girl was holding the muzzle of a high-powered rifle, only inches from Eli Lashe's right temple.

———··———

It's strange when I think about it. I clearly remember continuing to look straight at Taft and Granville before slowly turning to the right to look at his young wife. As you've heard people say, in that moment it was like things slipped into slow motion. Maybe I just didn't want to see what was there. Tate's face was filled with shock and Glanville's nothing but rage.

Tate held out both hands in something like a hold-on-now motion. What was shaping up to be no more than a difficult moment had suddenly become a matter of life and death. Sandra Granville was petite and she couldn't have been much taller than that rifle was long. She was trembling.

There were one or two other attempts by Tate to calm her down and several more shouts from her husband, "pull the trigger", "kill 'em both". I don't remember saying anything. I'm pretty sure I didn't. All I remember clearly doing was staring at the hole in the end of that rifle, which looked like the mouth on a 5-gallon bucket.

There was no such thing as a plan of attack. I didn't come up with some magical, persuasive words. That's only in the movies. What happened was quick and simple.

When she turned a little more toward Tate, I saw that the index finger on her right hand wasn't on the trigger. In fact, she had her entire hand wrapped around the stock behind the trigger guard. That's when I grabbed the barrel with both hands, held on as tight as I could and slung Sandra into her husband. Using a handful of rifle and a handful of hair I got her on the floor. Thankfully, she did more crying than fighting.

My partner immediately went after Lonnie. Tate Taft appeared to take out several years of frustrating lies and broken promises on Granville's head and shoulders.

If you figure in the fact it was a pleasant Sunday afternoon in June; the fact we were confronting a man Tate Taft had known for years; the fact that Tate didn't even have a brand new wife in his Lonnie Granville "equation"; and the fact that we were sitting down to talk about a violation not typically calling for the highest vigilance, some might agree our actions and inactions didn't rise to the level of rank incompetence. But the way we handled things that day has to at least make the "sloppy police work" folder.

Beginning that evening and continuing to this very day, I'm haunted by the fact that we went into that trailer to arrest a habitual offender and didn't even ask about anyone else being in the trailer, much less fully clearing the place.

Had Sandra Granville been older, more experienced with a weapon, or just meaner, things might have turned out very differently. The unexpected, by definition, comes when you least expect it. That day at Hughes Trailer Park two experienced officers ended up being far luckier than smart.

For the remainder of my law enforcement career Sheriff Earl Simpson's words were no longer part of some running joke. They were much closer to a guiding principle - "be on the lookout - for anything!"

DISPOSITION

There was no way the details of what happened in the Granville trailer could be kept to ourselves, although that's the way we would have preferred.

Earl Simpson was thoughtful to reprimand us in private. Even behind closed doors he chose to emphasize the department's policies and procedures, rather than scolding us personally. As much as anything, I was bothered by the thought I'd fallen short of his expectations. I've always felt the sheriff was more frightened for us than mad at us.

For another year or so, Detective Taft continued to be involved with Lonnie Granville. But that day in the trailer, seeing how readily his former friend could turn vicious, Tate stopped trying to help that character all together.

It turned out his young wife's family was more than a little angry. Sandra's older brother caught up with Lonnie in a beer store parking lot, and really bounced him around. The last I heard Tate say anything about it, his former football teammate was serving time in Mississippi.

In the days after the incident, Sandra Granville was charged with aggravated assault. Tate and I met with the prosecutor and the charge was subsequently reduced. The 17-year-old had gotten mixed up with a real greaseball, who jerked her life in the wrong direction, got her in trouble with the law and sent her back to Polumbo County pregnant. I was glad to see her receive only probation, and be allowed to return home to those who loved her.

> Comment: This wasn't the only time Eli Lashe tried to help someone he felt deserving of a second chance. Doing so brought him obvious pleasure.

ABOUT AS BAD AS IT GETS

April 21, 1968

In almost 25 years on the job I managed
to avoid any really serious personal injury. I
was also fortunate in that I never saw a
fellow officer severely injured or killed in
my presence.

Of course, that's not to say I didn't see
my share of pain and suffering. We all did. If
an officer patrols the roads and enforces the
law long enough, those particularly-trying
calls will come: highway accidents, murders,
hit-and-runs, drownings, suicides, child abuse,
deadly fires and more.

There are certain calls officers never
forget. There are always two or three stories
which stand out. For me, this is certainly one
of them.

On Saturday, April 21st, 1968 Chief Deputy
Dan Simpson was patrolling with me in the

Northeast corner of the county. It was, and still is, the most rural (even remote) part of Tuhont, with houses few and far between.

The lone exception was the Shallow Creek Community, where 15 to 20 families lived in 2 or 3 square mile area. The village had long been associated with a textile mill which closed in the 1940's. Back in the '60's, as they were from day-one, the houses were small and simple.

As was true in mill villages like Shallow Creek, a majority of the residents were law-abiding, hard-working people. However, the few that weren't stood out.

One such household was that of Titus and Jenelle Biggs. The neighbors' calls typically involved public drunk and disorderly conduct complaints about goings-on in and around the Biggs house.

That Saturday night in '68 the complaint came from the next door neighbor, and the specifics were alarming.

———··———

When the call came through, Eli and Simpson had just gotten back in the car after a meal at Dot's Seafood.

"Tuhont County to 1667..."

Lashe cranked the Pursuit Special before answering.

"Go ahead Tuhont."

"Eli, you anywhere near Shallow Creek?" asked Avery Cooley.

"We're just leaving Dot's Seafood. We can be there in about ten minutes. What ya got?"

"Titus Biggs' next door neighbor, Spencer Tomlin, just called and said we need to get a car to the Biggs' house as soon as possible. Tomlin said some kind of disturbance is goin' on."

Lashe turned and accelerated north on CR 2217 before asking for further clarification.

"County, what sort of disturbance, did he say?"

"Tomlin's wife was yelling in the background and it was hard to understand just what he was sayin'. But it was somethin' about one of the Biggs' children crying and screaming for a long time. Tomlin said he could hear Titus Biggs yelling 'shut up' at the child. He said both Biggs and his wife were drunk. It sounded like what

[213]

Spencer and his wife were listenin' to really had them shook up."

By the time Avery Cooley finished painting the picture of what might be happening in the Biggs house, the Fury Pursuit was wide open. Both Lashe and Simpson knew of Titus Biggs' temper and his habit of drinking most of the day on Saturdays. Those thoughts combined with persistent screams of a child had the makings of something bad.

———— ... ————

Although the call technically came from someone else, Dan and I agreed it would be best if we went directly to the Biggs home. Neither one of us really knew Spencer Tomlin, but there was no reason to think sending us to Titus Biggs' place was anything but on the up-and-up. It certainly wasn't the first time neighbors had called with complaints of fighting at that place.

When Dan and I pulled up, the house was dark, except for an uncovered bulb above the side door. Our headlights flooded the slate shingle siding, which was weathered, badly stained and broken away in several places

around the two bottom rows. There was a small
front stoop with broken cement steps tilting
in a couple of directions.

Like I've written previously, here's
another thing that stuck sort of firmly in my
mind that night one in Shallow Creek. What I
remember so clearly is the electric-blue paint
on the window frames. It only seemed to deepen
the contrast between something fresh-looking
and the drab, dilapidated look of everything
else....don't know why I noticed it so that
night, but I did.

I also remember the frantic barking of
the Biggs' dog, apparently as upset by the
sounds coming from inside the house as by the
arrival of two men in a car with flashing red
lights.

In short order, we were to discover that
the inside of Titus and Jenelle Biggs' house
made the outside look first-rate.

Lashe and Simpson had just gotten out of the Fury when the child screamed again. The chilling sound sent both officers hurrying toward the house, Lashe toward the front door and Simpson toward the side entrance.

Another scream was followed by the yell which had frightened the Tomlins so badly, "Shut up in there, and go to sleep! The command was harsh, slurred and filled with the angry tone often associated with drunkenness."

Lashe pounded on the front door, motivated by the continued cries of the child. "Mr. Biggs, it's the sheriff's department. Open this door! Open it, right now!"

Two more frenzied screams of what sounded more like a baby than a toddler, and Dan Simpson kicked in the side door. Everything in both officers told them the situation inside sounded like a matter of life and death. The baby's cries weren't "typical" in any sense of the word. They were filled with trembling, filled with the desperation that comes when a baby can't cry any harder.

———— ··· ————

Just as I heard Dan yell he was going in, I tried the door handle and found the door unlocked. As I went in the front room, my flashlight told a story I could hardly believe. The house was an absolute wreck. The stench was as bad as the look of the place - crumpled-up wrappers and food containers, empty beer bottles, soiled diapers in a large, plastic bucket and all manner of dirty clothes everywhere.

I've seen quite a few things in my time, each evoking its own brand of stress, but standing in that open door, looking at the way those people lived as backdrop for the terrible cries of that child brought on a moment of stress I can still feel.

Another scream from the room in the left rear corner sent us to the bedroom door. Dan found the light switch first and flipped it on.

When the room lit up, one of the large, brown rats was disappearing into a hole in the floor near the rusting baby bed. The other was running around on the mattress under what was left of a tattered pink blanket near the 10-month-old girl. Dan hit at the rodent twice with his club, but it too managed to escape and disappear into the same hole.

———··———

Lashe sat the little girl up in the bed and took a closer look with his flashlight. Simpson went to the broken plank to make sure the rats had gone.

"Oh, my God, Dan, look at this!" exclaimed Lashe, as he laid the baby back down on the mattress.

As both officers leaned over the bed rail, Jenelle Biggs stepped into the bedroom doorway just in front of Titus. "What the hell's goin' on here?" she demanded, looking and sounding every bit as belligerent and drunk as her husband.

Lashe whirled in their direction and drove both of the baby's parents into the far living room wall. Jenelle Biggs was sent to the floor and her husband was spun, handcuffed and unceremoniously escorted to the cluttered couch. Jenelle was simply too drunk to get up.

———··———

Dan and I felt the amount of blood on the baby and in the bed dictated we not wait on an ambulance. In the short time since we'd arrived, the little girl seemed to have almost

[218]

stopped crying and appeared to be growing listless.

I wrapped her in a blanket we had in the Plymouth and high-tailed-it for the emergency room at Tuhont County Hospital. Trying to comfort and keep an eye on the baby, while holding that powerful Fury on those crooked county roads made for an unnerving trip.

Dan stayed with the Biggs' until another unit could get to the house.

I would argue any officer who worked as long as I worked and says he or she never gave in to the over-powering impulses of rage and its demand for excessive force, is being dishonest both with themselves and their listeners.

That night in Shallow Creek it was smart that I take the child and Dan stay with those two. I'll never get the sight of the baby's heels out of my mind. She'd kicked them bloody against the metal rails, while the two rats ravaged her face, and her drunken parents yelled at her to "shut up". I still feel the flashes of rage when I talk about it.

> Comment: Millie Lashe told me she didn't like Eli telling this story. She said it still upsets him and makes him nervous, something I could see when he was retelling me the parts for the sections I prepared. No doubt, years later, he still carried the effects of that gut-wrenching experience.

DISPOSITION

After getting her to the hospital, I never saw Tricia Biggs again. But several years later others around town said the surgical work done in Atlanta was remarkable, given what the rats had done.

They took her bottom lip, several fingers, most of her chin, cartilage from both ears and part of one eyelid. A doctor friend of mine who was working in the ER that night

[220]

said what really got to him were the ragged
bites in the tip of Tricia's tongue.

Titus and Jenelle Biggs lost their
little girl to a foster home. The Biggs' were
convicted of child abuse and received what I
thought was very modest time. If you'd been
with Dan and me that night, you'd agree.

Wildlife officials said the rodents were
most likely large brown rats, a distinct breed
which can grow up to 10-inches long. I know
that awful night they looked more like
beavers to me.

THAT THIRD RACE IN '68
November 23, 1968

On the national and international
fronts, 1968 was a turbulent year. The Vietnam
War stirred peoples' emotions, leading to riots
on college campuses and in the streets of
America's larger cities.

Both Martin Luther King, Jr. and
presidential candidate Robert Kennedy were
assassinated. Richard Nixon was elected
President, after running a campaign in which
he promised to return law and order to
American cities and bring new leadership to
the Vietnam War.

Folks my age can well remember 1968 and
the deep divides in national politics.

Just as politics dominated the national
media, local papers and radio stations
reported on races being run in counties all
over the country.

[223]

One such race was for the sheriff's position in Tuhont County.

After 16-years of service and in declining health, Earl Simpson chose to retire. I remember so well the morning meeting where he told us of his plans. Many felt he might decide to do so, but it still came as a blow to most of us.

He'd done a solid job and earned the respect of just about everyone in Tuhont and the surrounding area. For years he'd been active in local civic clubs, serving one year as president of the Georgia State Sheriff's Association.

In the fall of '68, I couldn't help but feel Sheriff Simpson, struggling with worsening emphysema, just didn't feel up to taking on two tough opponents, both of which had made clear their intentions to run. He knew they would be formidable, one in particular.

At the time the sheriff decided to bow out, Dan Simpson hadn't announced his intention to run for the office his father was leaving. His wife, Trixie, wasn't big on the idea. She would have preferred Dan take the job her father had offered in his metal fabrication business.

But Earl's retirement and the opportunity it offered was more than Dan could resist. He announced the week after his father issued a written statement, making clear his intention to step down.

On November 5th, 1968, Dan routed both opponents, one by a 2-to-1 margin and the other close to 3-to-1. The people of Tuhont didn't just vote for Chief Deputy Dan Simpson, they clearly voted for a continuation of the law enforcement practices and reserved style

Earl Simpson had demonstrated over the previous 16-years.

That's why some of us were taken aback after the new sheriff made, what today might be called a proactive visit to the local drag strip just over two weeks after the election. It was Saturday night, November 23rd, the last event of the season, and the crowd was SRO.

In the sixties, teenagers and some well-beyond their teen years raced at three places in Tuhont County: a long, wide stretch of scenic highway just inside the county line northwest of Asheford; a recently paved and widened section of road used by 18-wheelers going in and out of International Milling's 100-acres, and at the Redline Dragway just south of Shallow Creek.

Our department did its best to confine the competition to the Redline track. As you might imagine, we weren't always successful.

Throughout the 1960's, muscle cars ruled.
Every major manufacturer had players: the
Ford's Mustang in all its variations,
Chevrolet's powerhouse Camaros, Chevelles and
souped-up Novas, Pontiac's GTO and Trans Am,
Buick's Wildcat and Skylark GS, the Oldsmobile
4-4-2 and Cutlass Ram-Rods, Plymouth's
Roadrunners, Dodge's Charger and the
surprisingly strong re-powered, push-button
Polara.

Shortly before the election, our
department took delivery on a new Charger
R/T. It had a 3-speed, console automatic
transmission, which I remember being very
strong and smooth.

The only things deleted on the order
were the bumble bee logo and bumble bee
stripes (two thin stripes framing two thick
stripes) around the rear on all of the R/T's.
Sheriff Simpson thought they would be a bit

much. The rest of us agreed. In addition, all of the show chrome was omitted at the factory.

Why a Dodge Charger in the middle of all those full-size Plymouth, Ford and Chevrolet police specials? The answer is simple. We needed something to keep up with the muscle cars.

It was probably the road-hugging look of the special suspension, the smooth, soft finish on the over-sized tires, along with the no non-sense feel created when the eyewash chrome was removed that did the trick.

———···———

Simpson, Lashe and Renea Raney agreed to meet at Redline's concession stand at 7:00 PM. Lashe and Raney were there ten minutes early, discussing the unique smell of a southern drag strip, a combination of popcorn, gasoline and burnt rubber, when track-owner Horace Baker's son, Eddie, walked up.

"Hey, deputies, where's the new sheriff at?"

"Hello, Eddie," replied Eli.

Raney didn't speak. Tuhont County's first female deputy barely looked in his direction. Baker's several brushes with the law and the nonchalant attitude he'd shown each time, left her unimpressed with the arrogant twenty-year-old.

He'd grown up around the straight track, owned more than his share of street rods and enjoyed a reputation for taking it to the streets. Many local officers believed it was Baker's mouthy goading that fueled local teenagers' determination to beat Eddie Baker on or off the track.

"I wanted to congratulate him on winning the sheriff's election. I thought that retired federal guy might have been better for the job, but Dan was absolutely my second choice," said Baker.

"Well, Eddie, I'm sure Dan will be sorry he missed you. But I'll tell him he almost made the top of your list. I'm sure he'll be troubled to hear he fell just short." Baker appeared to completely miss the sarcasm in Eli's reply.

After an insincere smile, he started to walk away with his noticeably older girlfriend, before quickly turning back toward the officers. "By the way, I hear you guys got a new hotrod Charger. I'm anxious to see it."

Comment: Eli tastefully left out the description of Baker's girlfriend I'd heard him offer on a couple of other occasions. He said she didn't seem to realize her time in pedal-pushers, a ponytail and an overdone wad of bubble gum, American Graffiti-style, had come and gone.

———••·———

[229]

I didn't know if Dan would want me to tell Baker, but I knew he was in the new Charger that night. Only moments after Eddie and his lady-friend walked away, our new Sheriff pulled up, and parked just outside the front gate, and I mean, just outside, the front gate. That was the first clue that Dan was up to something with our new muscle car. I just had no idea how far things would go.

We'd talked about staying at the track an hour or two. Dan wanted to thank some people he knew would be there for their support in the election. Over the course of several classes of competition folks stopped by to speak, many commenting on and asking about the Charger.

The three of us were about to leave when Eddie showed up again, alone. The talk almost immediately turned to the car. In short order all four of us were standing near the open driver's door. From the beginning, it was apparent the county's number one drag racer and 0-to-60 expert found the Charger to be some sort of challenge to his status by the local law.

Dan's calm demeanor in the face of Eddie's needling questions should have been a second clue to Dan's thinking about the statement he wanted it make in the heart of Tuhont's drag racing community.

———··———

"An old man's automatic, now what kind of transmission is that when you really want to get up and go? At least it's in the console and not hung out there on the steering column. Why didn't you get a 4-speed, Sheriff?"

"That automatic does alright. Tell you what Eddie, when you shower down on it you better have a plan. Know what I mean?" asked the new Sheriff with a wry grin.

"Now, what kind of horsepower did you say it has?"

"Three-seventy-five I believe they told me, with four-hundred-eighty foot pounds of torque. I knew you would want to know that," added Simpson.

[231]

Baker withdrew his head and shoulders from inside the driver's door. "Well, as you know, I'm really more of a General Motors man. I'm still waiting on someone that can handle that street-legal GTO of mine."

There was a moment of silence before Eddie Baker's face lit up.

"Hey, Dan, it's the last race night of the season. Let's give the crowd a real treat. Why don't you and I get out there and take a run down the old Redline quarter mile? Come on man, what cha think?"

Raney and Lashe looked at one another, unable to believe Dan Simpson's silence. There reaction was the same – surely, only two weeks into his new administration, he wasn't going to go tearing off down the Redline drag strip along side Tuhont County's most noteworthy drag racer – legal or illegal.

As surprised as they were with his failure to respond with an immediate – no! His next words almost floored them both.

"And, what you gonna say when I beat you in that unbeatable GTO?"

"Sheriff, that ain't no worry of mine, 'cause you ain't gonna beat me. Come on, let's see what our new Sheriff can do, him in his new county Charger and me in my GTO. My dad can get on the PA system and tell the folks we have something special for them right after the night's final event."

Lashe felt like he'd known Dan Simpson long enough to take a little liberty. He respectfully took the

[232]

Sheriff's arm and led him over to the chain-link fence. "What's ya thinkin', Dan? I don't know about this, you drag racin' in a piece of county equipment against that punk. He beats you and his influence over the teenagers in this county goes straight up."

Simpson listened silently, before looking up at Raney, who was standing behind Eddie Baker. She slowly shook her head from side to side. But Dan Simpson was nobody's fool. He understood the upside and downside of what he was considering. The new sheriff lowered his head, then looking up at the stands before offering his friend a smile.

"Two things here Eli, we've got to earn a little respect; they need to know if we want to, we can catch them; and that blowhard over there needs to be taken down a few notches. One good run and we might just accomplish both – right here, tonight, in that new Dodge of ours."

"You and I have given it a go. That thing will fly; all I've got to do is get the best it has to offer."

Lashe followed Simpson back to where Baker was standing. "Now, let me ask you a couple of questions about that canary-yellow GTO you're so famous for. What am I up against?"

"It's a 1965 Tri-Power three-eighty-nine. It's rated at three-hundred-eight horsepower, putting four-hundred-twenty-five pounds of torque into the rear end through a close ratio 4-speed transmission. But the biggest difference won't be in the power train Sheriff; the

[233]

difference is gonna be in the driver's seat," replied Baker, flashing the self-assurance for which he was so famous.

Dan paused again, rippling his fingertips on the Charger's hood.

"Okay, Eddie, you're on, but there's one stipulation."

"I've obviously got a lot to lose here tonight, more than just a quarter-mile race, and I want you to put something on the table."

"What's that?"

"In that pre-race PA announcement, I want the fans told, should you lose, you'll pay for a month's worth of newspaper ads, urging all local racers to compete only in track-supervised events – just like Eddie Baker has committed to do."

Now, it was Baker pausing to carefully consider his words. Simpson was sure his ego would rule the night, and it did.

"Alright, Sheriff, let's do it."

———···———

The announcement was made, just like the Sheriff had asked. After the last regularly-scheduled race of the night you could feel the electricity in the crowd as the appliance-white Charger and yellow GTO prepared to approach the line.

That night Dan was wearing a windbreaker and slacks, rather than his uniform. He left his badge, pistol and belt hardware with Renea. I remember her leaning over to me and saying, "At least he's not racing in uniform. That helps." We both were having trouble believing our eyes.

I whispered a little prayer, trying to keep it from being too obvious. Let me tell you though, I glanced over at Renea Raney and she was in full prayer mode. I don't believe Renea even stopped praying when Horace Baker walked up.

Eddie's dad was a good enough sort. He certainly made a success out of Redline Dragway, demanding both competitors and fans follow the rules. I'll never forget it. He leaned a little in my direction and asked,

"Reckon we oughta stop this before it starts?" I didn't say anything, but I remember shaking my head, more in disbelief about what was going on than in response to Horace Baker's question.

A couple of guys helped both drivers find the line. Of course, Eddie got there quicker and easier than Dan. They eased the Sheriff up and back several times. That's when I couldn't help lowering my head. I just knew there was going to be a huge political price to pay in the court of public opinion.

The lights hit green and the two cars jumped off the line, with the GTO grabbing a quick advantage. That's when Renea dropped her face in her hands with crossed fingers against each cheek. I suppose I was looking over at her because the first few seconds after that start, I couldn't make myself look at the track.

From back at the starting line I wasn't able to tell just when and where the Dodge passed the Pontiac - maybe two-thirds of the way down the run. I do remember seeing the GTO twitch each time Baker shifted gears.

Perhaps that was the difference - Eddie's three shifts versus the unbroken flow of power through the Charger's TorqueFlite 3-speed automatic. The GTO ran a respectable 14.4 but it fell well short of the 13.9 turned in by Sheriff Dan Simpson in that new Dodge Charger.

Comment: I've forgotten how many times Eli said he's watched the famous car chase in the movie, "Bullitt". It's a bunch! Watching the Dodge Charger R/T go against the Mustang Fastback driven by Steve McQueen must bring back very satisfying memories of a high-stakes night at Redline Dragway.

In 1968, I followed the presidential race between Richard Nixon and Hubert Humphrey. For all the obvious reasons I took great interest in the race for sheriff in Tuhont

County. But it was that third race which still captures my imagination - that race between a white Charger with blue letters on the door and that famous, soft-yellow GTO at Redline Dragway.

DISPOSITION

As agreed, Eddie Baker ran newspaper ads promoting the idea of keeping racing where it belongs - on the track. His father died 5 or 6 years after the famous race, and Eddie ended up doing a good job running Redline. He got to where he did a lot more managing and promoting than racing. I believe he sold out to a local investment group in the early 90's.

Renea Raney joined the department not long after I did and she always did a good job. A year or so after our nerve-racking night at the track, Renea married her long-time boyfriend, Chip Ladd. The last I heard Chip and Renea had a couple of children and were living in Norfolk, VA where he worked for a company involved in some type of marine research.

Sheriff Earl Simpson died in 1988 from pneumonia and other complications. As I've written here and said many times, he was a good man and a good friend. He taught me a lot about an even-handed approach to the law and law enforcement.

When I lost my leg in that automobile accident back in 1987, Dan Simpson was in his 19th year serving as Sheriff of Tuhont County. He retired one year later, rounding out a total of 30-years with the department in one capacity or another. As I write this, Dan and Trixie are retired and living in Apalachicola, FL. I believe their twin daughters also live somewhere in the sunshine state.

Believe it or not, following Dan's (the department's) win over the king of local drag racing, there was a noticeable reduction in race-related complaints from the citizens of Tuhont. It seemed Dan's strategy to take some momentum away from the young, street-racing crowd may have worked. The newspaper ads helped also.

And here's a little confession. That night at Redline Dragway Dan wasn't quite as reckless as it might seem. He fibbed a little. Eddie wasn't going up against a four-forty. He was racing Dodge's new four-twenty-six Hemi V8 a dealer friend in Atlanta had gotten the department. In his ego-driven haste to get on the track and make a monkey out of the new sheriff, he never even asked Dan to raise the hood.

But I'm happy to report Dan Simpson and Ed Baker later shared more than a few laughs over that third race in 1968.

www.ingramcontent.com/pod-product-compliance
Lightning Source LLC
LaVergne TN
LVHW051500080426
835509LV00017B/1850